How to Know
GOD'S
Will

How to Know
GOD'S
Will

What the BIBLE *Says*

Robert M. West

BARBOUR
PUBLISHING

Published by Barbour Publishing, Inc., P.O. Box 719, Uhrichsville, Ohio 44683, www.barbourbooks.com

Our mission is to publish and distribute inspirational products offering exceptional value and biblical encouragement to the masses.

Member of the
Evangelical Christian
Publishers Association

Printed in the United States of America.

*Affectionately dedicated to
my three daughters—
Kimberly, Rebekah, and Sarah—
who have been entrusted
with the will of God.*

Contents

1
Understanding the Will of God

Therefore do not be unwise,
but understand what the will of the Lord is.
EPHESIANS 5:17

From the time we are very young, other people tell us what to do. Our parents, teachers, and others—even older siblings—make many of our decisions for us.

My three daughters, now grown, let my wife and me know their feelings about who was in charge by the first three words that they learned to speak: *Mama, Dada,* and *NO!* And so the battle of the wills began.

Children instinctively want to do *their* will. They want to do what they want, immediately, without concern for what anyone else thinks. But children quickly become adults, and their turn to make important decisions arrives. As life becomes more difficult, many people actually *hope* for someone to tell them what to do.

Perhaps that's why you're interested in the subject of God's will. If so, you'll be glad to know that God is willing and waiting to help you know His will, showing you answers and direction for your life.

The answers you need are found only in God's Word, and it's to the scriptures this book will go. As you read, please keep an open Bible nearby. Check the references and consider what is said here to gain the full impact of what God has revealed about His will.

God's Word is a lamp to our feet and a light to our path (Psalm 119:105). When we decide to look to God and His Word for help, there is no need to look any further. We will have arrived at the right place, and we will not be disappointed.

Our Reason for Being

People frequently ask searching life questions such as, "Who am I? Why do I exist? Does my life have a special purpose?"

For the best answers, we go back to the very beginning—and learn we exist because of God's will. We are not the random products of evolution or cosmic accidents. God has specially created us, and those living in heaven praise Him for that:

> *"You are worthy, O Lord, to receive glory and honor and power; for You created all things, and by Your will they exist and were created."*
> REVELATION 4:11

The psalm writer David also marveled at God's creative work and honored God for his life, saying, "I will praise You, for I am fearfully and wonderfully made" (Psalm 139:14). We can join this chorus of praise, realizing that we also live and exist because of God's will.

The first question and answer of the Westminster Shorter Catechism—a doctrinal statement created in the seventeenth century to teach Christians the basics of their faith—addresses man's search for purpose in existence:

> *Question: What is the chief end of man?*
> *Answer: The chief end of man is to glorify God and enjoy Him forever.*

The subject of God's will is important to Him. It is primarily for *His* glory rather than our personal satisfaction, success, or pleasure. If we are not careful, we can forget this important truth.

Ephesians 1 states three times that God's work of salvation—which is according to His will (1:5)—is also "to the praise of His glory" (1:6, 12, 14). The apostle Paul, who wrote the book of Ephesians, taught in the book of 1 Corinthians that we should always live to honor God: "Therefore, whether you eat or drink, or whatever you do, do all to the glory of God" (10:31).

If we search our hearts and discover that our primary interest in God's will is self-centered, it may be that all we really want is God's blessing on *our will*. But real Christianity holds that learning and doing God's will is for His glory, not our own gratification.

Understanding God's Will

Ephesians 5:17, printed at the beginning of this chapter, commands Christians to "understand" God's will. A little background to this verse should prove helpful.

The apostle Paul, in Ephesians 4, begins a practical section that describes Christian living. Paul encourages believers "to walk worthy" of God's call to salvation (4:1). The word *walk* is used repeatedly in chapters 4 and 5, referring to the way a person should progress in the Christian life. If we are going to say that we are Christians, we should live our lives in a suitable way, one that complements such a privileged position.

This "worthy walk" of the Christian life is then described in the following ways:

- A *different* walk, that reveals an extreme makeover from the godless and evil lifestyle practiced before one becomes a Christian (4:17–19).

- A *loving* walk, similar to the kind of love displayed by Christ when He gave himself for us (5:1–2).

- An *enlightened* walk, which refers to developing a new moral and spiritual standard of living that is acceptable to the Lord (5:8–10).

- A *careful* walk, taking advantage of opportunities to serve Christ as evil erodes society's openness to the gospel, people's personal interest in Christ, even the diligence of believers (5:15–16).

13

- An *empowered* walk, being under the Holy Spirit's control as the source of strength to live this way (5:18; see also Galatians 5:25).

This is all connected to the subject of God's will in Ephesians 5:17, where Christians are warned not to be "unwise" by succumbing to the world's pressure and rejecting a Christian lifestyle. This is an important element of God's will, and to "understand the will of the Lord" means to learn, accept, and practice these truths.

Since we are actually commanded to *understand* God's will, it stands to reason that God's will can be known. This should encourage all of us—especially those who have great concern about their future.

Our Great Need

The story of humanity is characterized by self-centeredness. Advertising tells us to "have it your way!" People want good health and plenty of money, green traffic lights and an open parking space. We want low prices—and no lines at the checkout.

But real life isn't that easy. The book of Job

tells us, "Man who is born of woman is of few days and full of trouble" (14:1), and, "Man is born to trouble, as the sparks fly upward" (5:7). We've all been born into a sin-cursed world and face lives of continual trouble. Our problems are compared to an outdoor fire with burning sparks constantly rising in the hot air—with the potential to spread trouble elsewhere.

Jesus described man's plight by saying the people of His day were prone to wander, "like sheep having no shepherd" (Matthew 9:36). No one cared for their souls or provided for their deepest needs. They were alienated from God, and their lives were sinful. Today, most people— if they're honest—will admit that they have felt like a sheep without a shepherd. They have complicated their own lives with far too many bad decisions.

And yet the opportunities for making decisions just keep coming. Young people must think about furthering their education. Others are considering marriage and beginning their own families. Some couples are wondering how to maintain their marriages. Workers must adapt their career goals to an ever-changing economy. And still other people have had the devastation of serious illness or the death of a loved one forced upon them—with all of the choices that these hardships bring.

Many of our challenges are external—from outside of us. But scripture also tells of our inherent desire to control our own lives—and warns us against ignoring God when making our plans. In the following verses, we find important encouragement to trust *God's* guidance:

- *O LORD, I know the way of man is not in himself; It is not in man who walks to direct his own steps* (Jeremiah 10:23). No one states our need more clearly than the prophet Jeremiah. When he saw the results of his countrymen's continual bad decisions— choices that eventually brought God's judgment in the form of the Babylonian captivity—he made the confession of Jeremiah 10:23. The prophet knew that humans were born in sin and find it impossible to direct their lives in a way that ultimately produces blessing from God.

- *There is a way that seems right to a man, but its end is the way of death* (Proverbs 14:12). Sin has affected man's perception of right and wrong. Because of sin, people walk a dead-end road. Left to ourselves, we make decisions that seem right—but far too often we lead ourselves astray. In our bad choices, we reap what we sow (Galatians 6:7). Adam and Eve thought that eating the forbidden fruit was better than obedience to their Creator—and they lost paradise. Ananias and Sapphira convinced each other that lying was better than honesty—and lost their lives. Judas Iscariot calculated that thirty pieces of silver had more value than following Jesus—and lost his soul.

- *In those days there was no king in Israel; everyone did what was right in his own eyes* (Judges 21:25). In Israel's history, the period of the judges was a dismal period of moral and spiritual decline because of people's independent spirit. They "did their own thing." This final verse of the book of Judges explains just why things were so bad at that time: When it came to making life choices, people looked to themselves instead of God and His appointed leaders. The ancient Israelites had more interest in doing their own will than doing God's. Times of decision occur in all of our lives, and the question becomes, "Will we pursue our own will or the Lord's?" We can all be thankful that our Great High Priest, Jesus the Son of God, knows every detail of our lives—and is sympathetic to us. The author of Hebrews had repeatedly found God's help, and because of Jesus' trustworthiness, encouraged others to join him in approaching God with personal requests: "Therefore let us draw near with confidence to the throne of grace, so that we may receive mercy and find grace to help in time of need" (Hebrews 4:16 NASB). It is a wonderful privilege to come near the great God, especially for His assistance.

God, who dispenses mercy and grace, has also put many promises in writing for our encouragement while we wait for His help.

God's Great Promises

Promises are only as good as the person who makes them. In God's case, He is always faithful and completely powerful to fulfill His word.

God's promises find a home in the hearts of His children as they discover through Bible study and personal experience that He keeps His word. The famed evangelist D. L. Moody often wrote the notation "T & P" beside verses in his Bible. The characters were shorthand for "Tried and Proven." Moody had experienced God's faithfulness to keep His word—and so can we.

These "exceedingly great" promises (2 Peter 1:4) are so called because they come from the great God, because they achieve great things, and because they reach all believers.

They are also called "precious" (2 Peter 1:4) because they reveal God's loving concern for our personal well-being. He was under no obligation to us but still gave these valuable promises out of His great grace, through Christ's redeeming work.

As we seek the Lord's will and leading in our lives, we will come to view God's promises as "exceedingly great and precious," as well.

One well known promise concerns God Himself coming to our rescue when we fear the future: "Fear not, for I am with you; be not dismayed, for I am your God. I will strengthen you, yes, I will help you, I will uphold you with My righteous right hand. . . . For I, the LORD your God, will hold your right hand, saying to you, 'Fear not, I will help you'"(Isaiah 41:10, 13). This is a tender picture of the heavenly Father touching His children, calming their fears, and providing His help. And this is only one of many such promises in the Bible. Here are a few more from the Psalms.

- *The steps of a good man are ordered by the LORD, and He delights in his way. Though he fall, he shall not be utterly cast down; for the LORD upholds him with His hand* (Psalm 37:23–24). God takes great pleasure in overseeing and directing the lives of His righteous people. At times, even these people can stray from God's path and fall— because they are not yet perfect. But when they sin, God is pleased to restore them. Then they can resume their journey of walking with God and doing His will.

- *Delight yourself also in the LORD, and He shall give you the desires of your heart. Commit your way to the LORD, trust also in Him, and He shall bring it to pass* (Psalm 37:4–5). This promise involves a believer's enjoyment of God—He delights in our way, and we are to delight in Him! This delight molds our desires to conform to God's revealed will. As Saint Augustine prayed, "O Lord, grant that I may do Thy will as if it were my will, so that Thou mayest do my will as if it were Thy will." Too often, we're disappointed when God doesn't seem to provide what we want. In those times, we need to trust in His goodness and wisdom, believing that He knows and wants what is best for us. And then we wait.

- *I will instruct you and teach you in the way you should go; I will guide you with My eye* (Psalm 32:8). From this psalm of penitence comes a clear promise about God: He is our Instructor who teaches us His will. Viewing ourselves as students of God, we can humbly follow our Guide, realizing we live in His presence under His watchful eye.

The psalmist clearly believed these promises—and responded with joyful confidence: "You will guide me with Your counsel, and afterward receive me to glory" (Psalm 73:24). Notice the progression of the verse: God leads His people through His word ("Your counsel") through this life. Then, when this life ends, we will experience a glorious reception by God in heaven! God's will does have an ultimate destination.

This contrast between life on earth now and

life in heaven later is an important one. Time and again, we place far too much importance on this hectic, distracting life, neglecting thoughts of eternity. But the reality is that physical life is very brief. The question of knowing God's will involves only a tiny fraction of our eternal existence.

The apostle Paul makes the same comparison, saying, "the sufferings of this present time are not worthy to be compared with the glory which shall be revealed in us" (Romans 8:18). While living life on a sin-cursed earth, with all its uncertainties and sorrows, we must keep the promise of heaven and its incomparable glory in the forefront of our thinking. We'll have a home there soon.

When life on earth ends, so will our concerns about knowing God's will. The day we enter glory, we'll learn firsthand how God's will is done in heaven. And since we'll live to enjoy Him forever, we should begin now to learn what pleases Him.

How Is God's Will Done in Heaven?

In response to their request, "Lord, teach us to pray," Jesus gave His disciples a model prayer that we now know as the "Lord's Prayer." The third request of that prayer is for God's will to be done here on earth as it is in heaven.

God wants earth to be more like heaven, but we are far from that. To have a bit of heaven on earth means that we should do God's will in our own world just as the angels and departed believers do God's will in His presence. They perform God's will immediately, without complaint or debate. They pursue His will willingly, joyfully, completely, constantly, and with unity.

This is what we pray for ourselves and our world when we pray "Your will be done on earth as it is in heaven" (Luke 11:2).

Marveling at God's Will

Many people are exposed to the idea of God's will very early in their Christian lives, when they learn the Lord's Prayer. In the King James Version of the Bible, Matthew 6:9–10 reads, "Our Father which art in heaven, Hallowed be thy name. Thy kingdom come, *Thy will be done* in earth as it is in heaven" (emphasis added). And so begins our introduction to the vast and mysterious subject of God's will.

It's vast because of the amount of scripture devoted to the topic—and because it touches the life of every human being.

Humans will never fully comprehend the mysteries of God's will. Our questions are real and provocative:

- *How is it that God controls all things, with a plan unfolding according to His schedule—yet He gives human beings the right to exercise their own will and make their own plans according to their own schedule?*

- *How can a good and holy God permit evil and the horrors that exist on earth?*

- *What is man that God is mindful of him?*

24

This final question—posed by King David in Psalm 8:3–4—reveals the truth that God looks beyond the sun, moon, and stars to see and care for *us*. In a similar way, the apostle Paul marveled at God's immeasurable work in saving human beings. He wrote, "How unsearchable are His judgments and His ways past finding out!" (Romans 11:33).

God Himself provided the best perspective when He spoke through His prophet Isaiah: " 'My thoughts are not your thoughts, nor are your ways My ways,' says the LORD. 'For as the heavens are higher than the earth, so are My ways higher than your ways, and My thoughts than your thoughts' " (Isaiah 55:8–9).

Different Aspects of God's Will

Biblical phrases such as "the will of God," "the will of the Lord," and "His will" are used to describe different aspects of God's will. These aspects operate together without contradiction.

As with many biblical truths, we cannot fully comprehend every detail or answer every question about the topic—we must simply trust all that the Bible says about it. To better understand God's will, we must recognize the existence of three distinct aspects. Theologians identify these aspects differently, and what is suggested here represents a traditional perspective that will help you recognize the facets of God's will.

God's Will of Decree: His Sovereign Will

This is God's eternal and unchangeable plan for all that He has made and all that will come to pass. We have limited knowledge of God's will of decree.

Much of God's plan is hidden from mankind and is called "secret things" (Deuteronomy 29:29). Only certain future events are revealed in prophecy. The disciples learned that sometimes God places a No Trespassing sign over His secret things (Acts 1:6–7). They are revealed when they happen.

God ordains all events—but because He is holy, He is not the author of evil. He *permits* evil to accomplish His good and wise purposes, which are for His glory and our good. God's decrees make up His plan and always come to pass since He accomplishes them by His omnipotence.

Here are some Bible passages that refer to God's sovereign will:

- Ephesians 1:11 refers to the God "who works all things according to the counsel of *His will.*"

- In Isaiah 46:10, God says "*My counsel* shall stand, and I will do all *My pleasure.*"

- Daniel 4:35 states that God "does according to *His will* in the army of heaven and among the inhabitants of the earth. No one can restrain His hand or say to Him, 'What have you done?'"

The following verses show God's control of various elements of the universe and our lives to accomplish His purposes:

- He spoke the universe into existence (Psalm 33:8–9).

- He owns and reigns over everything (1 Chronicles 29:11–12).

- He controls the planets (Job 9:8–9).

- He oversees earth's elements (Amos 4:7–8).

- He has power over animals (Jonah 1:17).
- He controls the rise and fall of nations (Romans 13:1) and their political leaders (Proverbs 21:1).

- He limits the activity of Satan (Job 1:12).

- He directs the salvation of sinners (Romans 8:28–30).

- He makes us who we are (1 Corinthians 15:10) and determines the beginning and length of our earthly life (Job 14:1, 5).

When facing personal difficulties, many people remind themselves that God has not abandoned them by saying things like, "God is still on the throne" or "He's the potter and we are the clay." That means the God who created us is good, wise, all-knowing, and all-powerful, controlling all the events of our lives by His love.

God's Will of Desire: His Moral Will

This is God's revelation of right and wrong and of His desire that people live in obedience to Him. Some have called this God's *perceptive will* because it is revealed in the precepts of His word.

This aspect of God's will may or may not be achieved in people's lives since it depends on their response. It can be divided into two categories:

GOD'S WILL FOR THE LOST

God's desire is that everyone would believe and be saved. "The Lord is. . .longsuffering toward us, not willing that any should perish but that all should come to repentance" (2 Peter 3:9). Perhaps the most well-known verse in the Bible declares God's affectionate longing for humans: "For God so loved the world that He gave His only begotten Son, that whoever believes in Him should not perish but have everlasting life" (John 3:16).

GOD'S WILL FOR THE SAVED

The apostle Paul laid out God's will for the saved in a letter to Christians in the Greek city of Thessalonica: "Rejoice always, pray without ceasing, in everything give thanks; for this is the will of God in Christ Jesus for you" (1 Thessalonians 5:16–18). Though we will consider this subject in greater detail in chapter 3, here are several other passages that clearly indicate God's will for the saved:

- We are to offer ourselves totally to God (Romans 12:1–2).

- We are to be obedient to those in authority over us (Ephesians 6:5–8).

- We are to be sanctified morally (1 Thessalonians 4:3–5).

- We are to maintain a good public testimony as citizens (1 Peter 2:13–17).

- We are to trust God in times of suffering (1 Peter 4:19).

God's Will of Direction: His Providential Will

This aspect of God's will indicates His special plan for each believer's life—and it dominates the interest of Christians who want to understand their future and learn God's purpose for their life.

God's providential will is revealed gradually as our relationship to Christ deepens and we experience His working through all the events in our lives. We will examine this more closely in chapter 4, but here are several verses that address God's providential will:

- *You ought to say, "If the Lord wills, we shall live and do this or that."*
  JAMES 4:15

- *The Holy Spirit said, "Now separate to Me Barnabas and Saul for the work to which I have called them."*
  ACTS 13:2

- *"I will return again to you, God willing."*
  ACTS 18:21

- *"I know the plans I have for you, declares the LORD, plans for welfare and not for evil, to give you a future and a hope."*
  JEREMIAH 29:11 ESV

Pastor and writer George W. Truett, who served as president of the Southern Baptist Convention from 1927–29, once said, "To know the will of God is the greatest knowledge and to do the will of God is the greatest achievement."

Nineteenth-century British evangelist and author F. B. Meyer wrote, "If only the will of God were done on earth, as it is done in heaven, there would be peace between the nations, and love and happiness in all our homes. . . . It is because men will not do the will of God that things are as they are!"

Understanding God's will is not optional. It is commanded in the Bible. Acquiring and applying this knowledge reveals whether we are wise or foolish.

Our prayer:

You will guide me with Your counsel,
and afterward receive me to glory.
PSALM 73:24

Questions to Ponder:

1. In Revelation 4, when the twenty-four elders cast their crowns before God's throne, what do they say about God's will?

2. Can you recall (or discover) a promise from the psalms about God's guidance?

3. What does the Lord's Prayer (Matthew 6:9–13) say about God's will?

4. Can you name and explain three aspects of God's will?

2
Jesus and the Will of God

*"Then I said, 'Behold, I have come
(in the scroll of the book it is written of me)
to do Your will, O God.'"*
HEBREWS 10:7 NASB

After reading the title of this chapter, you might ask, "Why consider Jesus' life when we're trying to learn God's will for our own?" But the two subjects are closely related. Jesus' life is so significant we don't dare overlook the information we find in the four Gospels about what He believed, taught, and experienced in relation to God's will. As we study God's Word on the Lord's life, we'll earn a better understanding of God's will for *our* lives.

Because Jesus put God's truth into action perfectly, Christians are repeatedly called to imitate the Lord's example. He was the actual embodiment of God's will. For instance, when

Jesus served His disciples by washing their feet, He told them, "I have given you an example, that you should do as I have done to you" (John 13:15).

The apostle Peter, who did not respond well to mistreatment, learned that Christians should learn from the Lord's life by suffering in a God-honoring way. He said "For to this you were called, because Christ also suffered for us, leaving us an example, that you should follow His steps" (1 Peter 2:21). Fellow disciple John, Jesus' closest friend, wrote, "He who says he abides in [Jesus] ought himself also to walk just as He walked" (1 John 2:6).

From these texts the great nineteenth-century British pastor Charles Spurgeon advised, "Hang this question in your homes—'What would Jesus do?'—and then think of another—'How would He do it?' For what Jesus would do and how He would do it may always stand as the best guide for us."

As we read the Bible, we see the high priority the Lord Himself placed on His Father's will. Jesus was sent from heaven with a mission—and He was determined to finish His great work of seeking and saving the lost. That wouldn't be easy: Jesus encountered many obstacles of

His enemies—even from family and friends—which He overcame with great patience and persistence.

Let's get a closer look at what God the Father revealed about His Son, how the Son viewed the Father's will, and how we should imitate Jesus' example. We can break our study down into 1) the instruction He provided, 2) the opposition He received, and 3) the crucifixion He endured.

The Instruction Jesus Provided

In His hometown synagogue, Jesus led a public scripture reading which He announced was fulfilled in Himself. The passage read in part, "The Spirit of the LORD is upon Me, because He has anointed Me to preach the gospel to the poor" (Luke 4:18). One major aspect of the Messiah's ministry was teaching. When the people of one city tried to persuade Him to stay and continue teaching, He said, "I must preach the kingdom of God to the other cities also, because for this purpose I have been sent" (Luke 4:43). Jesus' teaching makes specific reference to God's will—especially in what He taught about Himself and what He taught about salvation.

What Jesus Taught about Himself

Jesus showed that the Old Testament scriptures contained much information about Him, in prophecies such as he quoted in Luke 4:18 above, which came from Isaiah 61:1–2. Jesus went on to explain Himself and his mission directly.

JESUS PLACED A HIGH PRIORITY ON GOD'S WILL

Jesus once told His disciples, "My food is to do the will of Him who sent Me, and to finish His work" (John 4:34).

This follows shortly after the well known story of Jesus and the woman at the well, a woman we might call "the bad Samaritan" for her immoral lifestyle. Jews normally avoided Samaria due to the prejudices of the day, but verse 4 states that Jesus "needed to go through Samaria" en route to Galilee. He was directed there for a divinely arraigned appointment to share the gospel with this woman and her community.

While Jesus sat alone at the well waiting for His disciples, He violated a cultural norm as a Jewish man by speaking publicly with a Samaritan woman. When they returned, the disciples were surprised—but they would learn that the value of souls outweighed the prejudicial practices of that day.

As the woman left Jesus, now carrying *living* water, the disciples were again surprised when Jesus told them He already had food. Having stated earlier that "Man shall not live by bread alone but by every word that proceeds from the mouth of God," Jesus spoke of a spiritual food—that of doing God's will in winning the lost. Obeying God's will satisfied and sustained Jesus. We could say it was His favorite meal!

JESUS WAS SUBMISSIVE TO GOD'S WILL

A day after walking on the water, Jesus told a crowd, "I have come down from heaven, not to do My own will, but the will of Him who sent Me" (John 6:38).

In heaven, God's will is done by everyone, without resistance or conflict. That's very different from life on earth.

Jesus' words and actions were so contrary to the religious thinking and traditions of the day that many people assumed He was acting independently from God—and violating God's will. But Jesus explained He'd been sent from heaven with authority for His mission. He was one with the Father in nature and will.

Jesus knew that doing God's will would result in His own great suffering. But knowing the horrible details of what He would eventually experience, Jesus still went forward in humility, trusting His Father completely (see Matthew 16:21).

JESUS HAD A CLEAR UNDERSTANDING OF GOD'S WILL

"This is the will of the Father who sent Me. . ." (John 6:39).

Jesus taught that He had come primarily to die in Jerusalem as a sacrifice for sinners. In John 6:39–40, verses which address God's sovereignty and human responsibility in salvation, Jesus defines God's will for Him specifically in this work of saving sinners.

Crowds had anticipated an earthly Messiah who would provide for them materially, heal them physically, and deliver them politically— but Jesus was offering Himself as spiritual food resulting in spiritual life. Jesus explained that every sinner the Father gave to Him would come to Him in saving faith. And Jesus' responsibility before God would be to:

- give eternal life to all believers (6:27–29, 40).

- not reject anyone who truly comes to Him (6:37–38, 44).

- not lose any of them spiritually (6:39).

- resurrect them physically in the future (6:39–40).

In addition to His understanding of God's will, Jesus had a clear view of God's timing. Throughout His ministry, He spoke repeatedly of "His hour" as having not yet come. But as His death on the cross drew near, Jesus began to say, "The hour has come" (John 12:23). The Lord had no uncertainty about what He needed to do and when He needed to do it. His mission statement was clear.

JESUS WAS COMMITTED TO DOING GOD'S WILL

In John 8:29, Jesus said, "The Father has not left Me alone, for I always do those things that please Him." From His first recorded words at age twelve ("I must be about My Father's business" in Luke 2:49) to the cross where He announced

"It is finished" (John 19:30), Jesus was devoted to doing God's will.

God's own voice affirmed this truth at Jesus' baptism in Matthew 3:17 and then at His transfiguration in Matthew 17:5 when humans heard these words: "This is My beloved Son, in whom I am well pleased." Though Jesus had been criticized and accused by the religious leaders of the day, God wanted everyone to know that He was pleased with His Son's life.

Jesus knew that understanding God's will is only part of the equation. The more important part is *doing* God's will. Theologian and writer J. I. Packer emphasized that combination in the title of his book of devotions, *Knowing and Doing the Will of God.* Jesus was clearly dedicated to both.

What Jesus Taught about Salvation

To correct misunderstandings about the salvation God offers all people, Jesus clarified two things: 1) that being accepted by God into heaven requires more than a person's outward claim of following Christ, and 2) that being part of God's family surpasses all earthly ties.

A PROPER RESPONSE IS REQUIRED

"Not everyone who says to Me, 'Lord, Lord,' shall enter the kingdom of heaven," Jesus said, "but he who does the will of My Father in heaven" (Matthew 7:21).

In this verse, doing the Father's will is specifically related to accepting *God's* way of salvation—which has always been according to His mercy and grace. This warning was designed to shock those people who were trying to earn salvation by their good deeds, those going through the outward motions but neglecting the inward conversion of their hearts.

In Jesus' time, as in ours, some people were active in religious activity, quick to pledge allegiance to the Lord and talk about what they were doing. But as Jesus revealed in His parable of the two builders (Matthew 7:24–27), they had built their house—that is, their lives—on sinking sand. Choosing the false hope of self-righteousness, they had bypassed the solid rock of receiving true righteousness through faith in Christ alone. Accepting Jesus by faith was doing God's will!

To those who determined to work their way into salvation, Jesus explained in John 6:29, "This is the work of God, that you believe in Him whom He sent."

A SPIRITUAL FAMILY IS ACQUIRED

Jesus also said, "Whoever does the will of My Father in heaven is My brother and sister and mother" (Matthew 12:50).

When we accept God's salvation, beginning a life of obedience to His word, we receive new status as part of God's family. Jesus' comments were surprising, especially to His natural family. But since He always displayed love toward them, this was simply a way to teach His disciples of the unique spiritual relationship Christ has with true believers—a relationship that transcends the natural and biological ties of human families. Interestingly, the Lord's biological half-brothers—unbelievers at this time—would eventually become His spiritual brothers (see John 7:5; Acts 1:14).

Historically, Jews believed that the divine blessing of this relationship was restricted primarily to their own people. But by using the term "whosoever" (KJV), Jesus extended God's salvation to everyone. The apostle Paul would later explain that our earthly identities of race, social status, and even gender would give way to a new spiritual unity through our faith in Christ (see Galatians 3:26–28).

The Opposition Jesus Received

Anyone who decides to do God's will can expect trouble from other people. Some of them simply don't understand God's will for our lives; others have no interest in pleasing God at all. Opponents will try to subvert God's plan and if that doesn't work, may try to change what we believe about God's will for our own lives. Usually, the devil is directing this opposition behind the scenes. This was true in Jesus' life, as He experienced resistance from enemies, but also from friends and family.

Opposition from His Enemies

We would expect trouble from our enemies. Throughout the Bible, the archenemy of God and His people is a fallen angel, the devil, who directs demon forces to oppose God's work. The devil also entices people to oppose us as we seek to obey God.

The devil's opposition to Jesus was obvious from the moment of the Lord's birth. Revelation 12:4 indicates that the devil, identified here as "the dragon," continued his war against God by attempting to destroy God's Son when He became incarnate. In Matthew 2, the evil

King Herod, obviously influenced by the devil, planned to kill the babies of Bethlehem in an attempt to eliminate Jesus. Satan's hope was to stop God's plan of redemption.

Years later, as Jesus began His public ministry, God's Spirit led Him into a confrontation with the devil. In the wilderness, Satan tempted Jesus to pursue rulership of the world—while avoiding the agony of death on the cross (see Matthew 4:8–10).

Jesus withstood Satan's temptation, but the devil didn't give up. For example, Jesus faced various types of persecution, which eventually led to a plot to kill Him (see Luke 4:28–30; John 11:53).

The devil's hostilities against Christ and His followers were continual. We can expect the same treatment from Satan today.

Opposition from His Family

The strongest ties most people have in life are with their family. So it is very disappointing when our own family resists our efforts to do God's will.

Jesus' family took opposition to an extreme. As He began His new ministry, Jesus' family thought He was mentally deranged. Mark 3:21 states, "They went out to lay hold of Him, for they said, 'He is out of His mind.'"

We can imagine that Jesus' family meant well—but they completely missed who Jesus really was and the will of God for Him. From their perspective, Jesus had suddenly left the family carpentry business to become an itinerate preacher, dependent on others for support. Scribes had even accused Jesus of being demon possessed (see Mark 3:22). His family concluded it was time for an intervention—but Jesus continued daily doing His Father's will.

Opposition from the Crowds

The people who had experienced the "feeding of the five thousand" were so impressed with Jesus' supernatural abilities that they properly concluded He was the Messiah. But they were impatient—and rather than waiting for their promised national deliverer to be crowned, they planned to take matters into their own hands. They wanted to make Jesus their king by force.

The Jews were thinking of the immediate benefit to their nation. But for Jesus to establish His prophesied reign at that time would have violated God's plan—which included the humiliation of suffering and death before Jesus' exaltation (see John 6:15; Philippians 2:8–11).

Jesus' own disciples may have felt that the Lord's recognition was overdue. But Jesus neutralized the situation by dismissing His disciples, sending them to the next town, and then dispersing this fervent crowd. So the devil's old temptation of a crown without the cross, coming this time through a different channel, was foiled again.

Opposition from His Disciples

At least twice Peter, one of the Lord's closest friends, tried to change God's plan regarding Jesus' suffering and death. Like many people, Peter thought his own plan would be better than God's.

In Matthew 16, as Jesus began preparing His disciples for His death and resurrection, Peter became Satan's spokesman, trying to discourage the Lord from fulfilling His mission to provide redemption for sinners through His blood. The devil is always seeking allies for his schemes—and on this occasion found the unsuspecting Peter. Jesus' startling rebuke to Peter was, "Get behind Me, Satan!" (see Matthew 16:21–23).

On the second occasion, Peter used violence to defend the Lord from arrest—and was again rebuked by Jesus. The Lord explained that if He *wanted* to be rescued, thousands of powerful angels were awaiting His call to arms. The twelve disciples could be replaced with twelve legions of angels, but only if it was God's will to protect Jesus in that way. The evil events of this day in Jesus' life were part of Old Testament prophecy—and Peter was not to interfere with God's plan (see Matthew 26:51–54).

Who Killed Jesus?

Here's the Bible's answer:

God the Father: "The LORD has laid on Him the iniquity of us all" (Isaiah 53:6).

God the Son: "I lay down my life that I may take it up again. No one takes it from me, but I lay it down of my own accord" (John 10:17–18 ESV).

God the Spirit: "Christ, who through the eternal Spirit offered Himself without spot to God. . ." (Hebrews 9:14).

Satan: "The LORD God said to the serpent. . . He shall bruise your head, and you shall bruise His heel" (Genesis 3:14–15).

Roman leaders: "The rulers were gathered together against the LORD and against His Christ" (Acts 4:26).

The Jews: "Let all the house of Israel know assuredly that God has made this Jesus, whom you crucified, both Lord and Christ" (Acts 2:36).

All sinners: "Christ died for our sins according to the Scriptures" (1 Corinthians 15:3).

The Crucifixion He Endured

Age-old questions about suffering and God's will resurface as we consider the end of Jesus' earthly life. He experienced the disappointing unfaithfulness of His disciples, the angry rejection of the crowds, and the incredible injustice of the authorities which led to His horrible death.

Was all of this God's will? How did Jesus react to those who mistreated Him? What was His attitude toward God in all of this? The answers to these questions stand as a monument to Jesus' greatness—and we can learn important lessons from these trials in our Lord's life.

Jesus' Time in Prayer

When Jesus realized that the hour of His death drew near, He went to a favorite place to pray. Throughout the Lord's perfect life He is represented as a man of prayer, and this was especially true when He faced difficulties. Prayer was not His last resort but a priority and came natural to Him. He had taught His disciples how to pray by instruction and by His example.

A PRAYER OF VICTORY

"I have glorified You on the earth," Jesus prayed. "I have finished the work which You have given Me to do" (John 17:4). This chapter in John's Gospel contains Jesus' longest recorded prayer in the Bible, spoken just before His passion began in the Garden of Gethsemane. In Jesus' mind, His sacrificial death was essentially done. He had completed everything up to that hour that would bring glory to his Father. The events that would lead to His death had been put into motion.

A PRAYER OF SUBMISSION

Having entered the Garden of Gethsemane to pray privately before His arrest, Jesus said, "O My Father, if it is possible, let this cup pass from Me; nevertheless, not as I will, but as You will" (Matthew 26:39). He was "deeply distressed" and "sorrowful, even to death," as He anticipated drinking the cup of God's wrath. Awaiting abandonment by His friends, torture and death at the hands of His enemies—and, worst of all, the forsaking and punishment of His Father for our sins—Jesus still expressed in His prayer a trusting, uncomplaining submission to God's will.

Jesus' Time in Court

Jesus was arrested late at night then illegally examined through the night. Jewish religious leaders questioned the Lord three times then took Him to Roman civil authorities to be judged three more times. Jesus' interrogation before the Roman governor Pilate—who reserved the right to order capital punishment—was revealing.

THE INTERROGATION

After separate sessions of questioning Jesus, Pilate announced each time, "I find no fault in Him" (John 18:38, 19:4, 19:6). Jesus then began an unusual silence that surprised Pilate. When the governor said he possessed authority to condemn or release Jesus, the Lord answered, "You could have no power at all against Me unless it had been given you from above" (John 19:11). The question now before the court was this: Who was ultimately in charge of these unjust proceedings—Pilate or God? The governor seemed to grasp a sense of divine accountability and continued his feeble attempts to release Jesus. In spite of all the unfairness and abuse, Jesus maintained the quiet dignity of submission to God's will.

THE VERDICT

"Pilate gave sentence. . .he delivered Jesus to their will" (Luke 23:24–25).

The crowd was loud and fierce as Jewish leaders stirred the people to demand that *their* will be done and Jesus be crucified. Saying Pilate was unfaithful to Caesar if he released Jesus (see John 19:12), the people manipulated the governor into sentencing Jesus to be executed. In the end, Pilate tried to ease his conscience by literally "washing his hands" of matter—though his sin remained. Pilate then committed Jesus to the will of the people who had misjudged Him. Jesus, meanwhile, "committed Himself to Him who judges righteously" (1 Peter 2:23).

Jesus' Time on the Cross

As Jesus was nailed to a cross, unbelieving bystanders mistakenly thought God was punishing Him for false teaching and claims to deity. The prophet Isaiah had predicted this flawed thinking centuries earlier: "We esteemed Him stricken, smitten by God, and afflicted" (Isaiah 53:4).

But Isaiah then explained what was really happening: "He was wounded for our transgressions, He was bruised for our iniquities; the chastisement for our peace was upon Him, and by His stripes we are healed" (Isaiah 53:5). In what appeared to be Jesus' moment of defeat, the crowd would hear His cry of victory, "It is finished."

Those near the cross may have thought Jesus was saying His suffering was finished—but what He meant was that His divine mission, to offer His perfect life as a perfect sacrifice for sin, had been completed. In Greek, this statement is only one word, *tetelestai,* which, as it appears on ancient receipts, can indicate "paid in full." When Jesus spoke this word from the cross, He declared that His work of redemption was complete.

Redemption denotes the idea of setting someone free by the paying a price. That's exactly what Jesus did for us. Peter explains, "You were... redeemed. . .with the precious blood of Christ" (1 Peter 1:18–19).

At Calvary, God's will had been done. Jesus' mission—to die a sacrificial death—was now complete. Having entrusted His entire life to His Father, there remained only one final thing to do. Jesus said, "Father, 'into Your hands I commit My spirit'"(Luke 23:46), then breathed His last. Born as no other, having lived as no other, Jesus finally died as no other.

The Belief of the Early Church

Soon after the risen Jesus ascended to heaven, Christians made it clear what they believed about God's will in relation to the events leading up to Jesus' death. Their doctrine was not novel but based on truths in the Old Testament. We can see what they believed both in what they preached publicly and what they prayed privately.

What Early Christians Preached

In Jerusalem, at the time of a Jewish harvest festival known as the Day of Pentecost, the apostle Peter preached a powerful gospel sermon. In it, he described how the antagonistic crowd treated Jesus: "This Man, delivered over by the predetermined plan and foreknowledge of God, you nailed to a cross by the hands of godless men and put Him to death" (Acts 2:23 NASB).

According to Peter, the Crucifixion was no accident. God was well aware of the evil that was occurring and even permitted it, because by His infinite wisdom He had *planned* it all. These early Christians clearly believed in a great mystery—that the holy God, who could not sin, could preordain the evil actions of sinners then hold them accountable for their sinful behavior.

God did not force the crowds to do what they did but allowed them to make their own voluntary choices.

Peter then indicted the Jews for pressuring the Romans, who as "godless men," performed the crucifixion. The audience's response to Peter's sermon was amazing—three thousand people believed and were baptized.

What Early Christians Prayed

The prayers of the early church were an expression of what they believed and matched their public message. In response to persecution from the Jewish chief priests and elders for the apostles' preaching that Jesus had risen from the dead, the believers prayed, again emphasizing God's sovereignty in the sinful murder of Jesus: "Truly against Your holy Servant Jesus, whom You anointed, both Herod and Pontius Pilate, with the Gentiles and the people of Israel were gathered together to do what ever Your hand and your purpose determined before to be done" (Acts 4:27–28).

Once again, individuals and groups were identified for the evil roles they played in Jesus' death. Their voluntary sinful actions were permitted under God's sovereign control, as a part of His plan. And in spite of the Jewish leaders' opposition to their message, the disciples were not intimidated, but rather emboldened—believing that God was also in control of their lives.

Years ago, I heard a missionary who served in a dangerous location say, "The safest place to be is in the center of God's will." David Livingstone, the nineteenth-century Scottish missionary to Africa, once said, "I am immortal until the will of God for me is accomplished." Jesus' disciples seemed to believe this way, too, and pressed forward with God's will as their risen Lord had done.

God has provided the perfect example—the life of His Son—to show us how to know and do His will, even in the face of opposition and suffering. Jesus' life will always stand as a visual aid of how God's will is to be done on earth as it is in heaven. And Jesus lives today to help us finish our earthly lives with joy, having completed the work our Heavenly Father has also given us to do.

Our prayer:

Teach me to do your will, for you are my God!
Let Your good Spirit lead me on level ground!
Psalm 143:10 esv

Questions to Ponder:

1. What primary task did Jesus identify as God's will for His life?

2. Who opposed Jesus as He tried to do God's will?

3. What did Jesus teach about God's will and the salvation of sinners?

4. Who was responsible for the death of Jesus?

3
Christian Living and the Will of God

This is the will of God in Christ Jesus for you.
1 Thessalonians 5:18

We now arrive at the second aspect of God's will, which we can call His "will of desire." Some have called this God's "moral will" because it reflects His holy nature and His immutable standard of right and wrong. Still others have classified this as God's "preceptive will" because it is discovered in the numerous precepts of His written word. Whatever we call it, every believer can agree that the will of God is in the word of God for the people of God who are led by the Spirit of God.

A clear difference exists between God's sovereign will and His moral will. With God's sovereign will, we have total certainty that everything God has ordained in His creation will come to pass. But God's moral will, the good that God *desires* to happen, is dependent upon people—using their own will—deciding to do what God wants. God's moral will was embodied for all to see in the perfect life of the Lord Jesus. But as evil men grow worse and worse in our sin-saturated time, this particular aspect of God's will is not always found in our world.

When Christians live out God's will of desire, they are remarkably similar—no matter where they live in the world. Believers of different nations exhibit noticeable differences in clothing, customs, physical features, and language, but when they follow "the will of God in Christ Jesus" they are clearly all God's children. True believers all strive to follow the message Jesus taught and imitate the life He lived by the power He provides.

If you are concerned about knowing God's will for your life, here is good news: God is not hiding His will. In fact, He's trying to show it to us.

Most of God's will for our lives has already been revealed in the pages of the Bible—we just need to learn and live it. He has given us His written word as revelation, gifted teachers for our instruction, and His Spirit for illumination, direction, and power. God truly wants the best for everyone, and He's provided all we need to experience it.

More than three thousand years ago, Moses described both God's sovereign will (which is often unknown to humans) and his moral will (which can be known): "The secret things belong to the LORD our God, but those things which are revealed belong to us and to our children forever, that we may do all the words of this law" (Deuteronomy 29:29).

God reserves knowledge of many things to Himself alone. He may or may not reveal such knowledge to us at His own discretion. For example, He has provided some information about future events in the prophetic sections of the Bible. But God's will regarding our lives in the present is quite clear. It involves knowing and obeying His written instructions.

In the Bible, God has assigned moral boundaries within which believers can travel safely on their journey to glory. As the psalm writer said, "Your word is a lamp to my feet and a light to my path" (Psalm 119:105). Phrases such as "being in God's will" or "being out of God's will," then, become references to personal obedience or disobedience to God's word.

Avoiding Errors

Before we consider the specifics of God's moral will we should beware of certain errors that arise in reference to God's word, God's leading, and God's answering of prayers. A correct view of these matters will help us stay on track as we seek God's direction.

Misinterpreting God's Word

The Bible is our only source of knowledge regarding God's moral will—which raises the issue of properly understanding and applying God's word. Only then are we doing God's will.

On a Christian radio call-in program, a woman seeking marital advice explained that she felt God was leading her to separate from her husband, with whom she wasn't getting along. She quoted 1 Corinthians 7:15 as justification, saying "The Bible says that God has called us to peace and the only way I'll get some peace is if I leave him!"

This woman clearly hoped for agreement from the program host who, thankfully, *disagreed*. Did this caller believe she was truly doing God's will as recorded in the Bible? She clearly misunderstood what God meant, because she had improperly interpreted scripture.

What mistakes had this woman made? First, she made the common but serious error of ignoring the *context* of 1 Corinthians 7:12–16. This passage is not addressed to Christian couples but explains how a believer should live with an unbelieving spouse. Second, this woman made an even larger mistake by disregarding the *content* of the verse she quoted. 1 Corinthians 7:15 lays out the proper course of action if a Christian's unbelieving mate decides to end the marriage. In that case, the believer is to "let that person go" because "God wants us to live in peace."

If you're primarily interested in God's will regarding your own future, the idea of learning and obeying God's word may be the last thing you want to hear. But God's will is found in God's word—and His plan for all of our lives begins with His moral will as described in scripture.

To help us better understand it, we have divided the doctrine of God's will into different aspects. But always remember that these aspects are vitally connected. To discover God's individual will for our lives we must first learn to obey His moral will. As preacher and writer

Haddon Robinson has commented, "If you want God's will for the future, start living it for today."

Misunderstanding the Spirit's Leading

One of the Christian's great blessings is guidance from God's Spirit. In fact, as Romans 8:14 indicates, the Spirit's guidance is proof of our relationship to God the Father.

Unfortunately, some claim their decisions are the result of God's leading when their actions actually repudiate God's word. Religious overtones often camouflage our disobedience.

God never contradicts Himself. And since His Spirit directed human authors in the writing of scripture, God would never lead people in ways contrary to His written word. The Spirit of God uses the word of God to guide us.

That's why the psalmist prayed, "Direct my steps by Your word, and let no iniquity have dominion over me" (Psalm 119:133). All believers can expect God's leading, but when our decisions and actions are contrary to scripture, we should expect God's *opposition*. Hebrews 12:5–11 calls this *chastening*, which is another indication of genuine sonship.

Bible scholar William Hendriksen has

said, "When the Holy Spirit leads believers, He becomes the controlling influence in their lives, bringing them at last to glory." It is "by the Spirit" that we put to death the deeds of the flesh (see Romans 8:13). It is God Himself who produces the first fruits of the Spirit in our lives (see Romans 8:23). So we must be clear: If people are disobeying God's word, they are *not* being led by God.

Misusing Prayer

Proper prayer plays a vital role in our learning and doing God's will.

We've all heard clichés like "prayer changes things" and "prayer changes us," but understand that prayer never changes God's moral will. We accomplish nothing by "praying" over a matter while violating God's word.

To say "I prayed about it" doesn't guarantee that we are doing God's will. Our prayers never supersede God's word. Always remember that obedience is a condition for answered prayer: "And whatever we ask we receive from Him, because *we keep His commandments* and do those things that are pleasing in His sight" (1 John 3:22, emphasis added). When God has conveyed

His desires in scripture, the only prayer we need is found in Psalm 143:10: "Teach me to do Your will, for You are my God."

Let me offer three examples of inappropriate prayers for God's will:

- When I happened across someone who had attended one of my Bible classes years earlier, I asked how the person's spiritual life was going. I was told that my former student hadn't been to church in a long time and was praying about returning. *Praying about it?* I thought. Yes, in one sense, we should pray all of our spiritual weaknesses—but the prayer needed here was the confession of not assembling with believers to worship (see Hebrews 10:25).

- Married people don't have to pray about whether to have an affair. God has clearly revealed His will about this in His word. Anyone considering such a choice should confess the sinful desire and then act accordingly—by avoiding the source of temptation.

- The story of the "prophet for rent" Balaam in the book of Numbers is an example of someone who put a love of money over the revealed will of God. When Balaam prayed, God made His will very clear (22:9–12). That should have settled the matter for Balaam. But when the stakes were raised, Balaam was determined to have his own way—so he prayed again (22:19). This time, God let Balaam have his own sinful way (22:20). The prophet followed a way that seemed right to him, but the result was ultimately fatal (see Numbers 31:8).

God's Will: For the Lost

Now we turn to God's clearly revealed will, as it relates to those who have not received Jesus as Savior.

Jesus Himself warned of the sad reality that some people will not end up in heaven: "Wide is the gate and broad is the way that leads to destruction, and there are many who go in by it" (Matthew 7:13). He explained in John 3:16 that if sinners don't believe in Him, they will "perish"—a word which is immediately defined as being "condemned" (John 3:18) and under "the wrath of God" (John 3:36). In another passage, Jesus indicated this is an eternal condition (see Matthew 25:46). And it is for this reason that God, out of His great love, "gave His only begotten Son."

God has repeatedly referred to Himself in scripture by the title "Savior." He longs for lost sinners to be rescued from the coming punishment, and aches when even the wicked perish (see Ezekiel 18:23, 32). As the apostle Peter said, answering the criticism of unbelievers who scoffed at the seeming failure of the Lord's promised return, "The Lord is not slack concerning His promise, as some count slackness, but is longsuffering toward us, not willing that any should perish but that all should come to repentance" (2 Peter 3:9).

The apostle Paul also confirmed this, speaking of "God our Savior, who desires all men to be saved and to come to the knowledge of the truth" (1 Timothy 2:3–4).

Not surprisingly, Satan actively opposes God's desire by promoting false ideas of salvation. Let's consider three of the devil's misconceptions:

- Some people believe that "being religious" makes them right with God. In the Gospel of John, the pharisee Nicodemus fell prey to this flawed thinking. A national spiritual leader who observed rituals, rules, and traditions, he was also a moral man with a reputation as a great teacher in Israel. But Jesus told Nicodemus that unless he was "born again" he would not see the kingdom of God! He was religious—and lost. But God wanted Nicodemus to be saved, so Jesus explained this "new birth" as something produced in us by the Spirit when true faith is placed in Christ alone (see John 3:6–7, 15–18).

• Some people think they are acceptable to God because of their heritage. Jesus dealt with this error when He questioned some Jews' relationship to His heavenly Father. "We are Abraham's descendants," they told Jesus. "Abraham is our father" (John 8:33, 39). Jesus' sad diagnosis was that the devil was their spiritual father (John 8:44). In doing the devil's will, they had, as the Gospel writer Luke reported, "rejected the will of God for themselves" (Luke 7:30). Understand that this problem is not limited to a particular race at a particular time—today, we must not think we become

God's children genetically. Salvation is not passed on to us when we are born to our parents. We are not part of God's family just because our parents believed. It's been said that God has children but not grandchildren!

- Some people simply assume that they don't need to concern themselves with spiritual things. Like those in the apostle Peter's time who said "all things continue as *they were* from the beginning of creation" (2 Peter 3:4), they tell themselves that God hasn't yet invaded human history with His judgment—and never will. Peter, though, corrected that kind of thinking by reminding these people of three things: the global flood of Noah's day, God's unique view of time, and what God really desires—their salvation (see 2 Peter 3:3–9).

For God's will to be done, these kinds of errors must be rejected and Christ—who calls Himself "the truth"— must be received. "But as many as received Him, to them He gave the right to become children of God, to those who believe in His name" (John 1:12). Receiving God's gift of eternal life is where Christian living begins. Then, "He who does the will of God abides forever" (1 John 2:17).

God's Will—For the Saved

The book of Psalms begins with these words: "Blessed is the man who walks not in the counsel of the ungodly, nor stands in the path of sinners, nor sits in the seat of the scornful; but His delight is in the law of the LORD, and in His law he meditates day and night" (Psalm 1:1–2).

God reveals His will in His word, through positive instruction about what to do or negative warnings about what to avoid. In studying the Bible, we will many times discover that scripture speaks directly to the situations we face. On other occasions, when God's word does not specifically address our circumstance, there are still plenty of general principles to follow—commands that will provide the direction we need and the confidence we want to know how to please God.

At times, God has summarized His moral will into a few basic expectations. In the days of Moses, for example, God's will was summed up in the Ten Commandments. And this rhetorical question was put to the generation about to enter the promised land: "What does the LORD your God require of you, but to fear the LORD your God, to walk in all His ways and to love Him, to serve the LORD your God with all your heart and with all your soul, and to keep the commandments of the LORD and His statutes which I command you today for your good?" (Deuteronomy 10:12–13).

Centuries later, Solomon, the wisest and wealthiest of kings, when considering the significance of man's life on earth, said, "Let us hear the conclusion of the whole matter: Fear God, and keep His commandments: for this is the whole duty of man. For God shall bring every work into judgment, with every secret thing, whether it be good, or whether it be evil" (Ecclesiastes 12:13–14 KJV).

The Lord Jesus summarized God's will this way: " 'You shall love the LORD your God with all your heart, with all your soul, and with all your mind.' This is the first and great commandment. And the second is like it: 'You shall love your neighbor as yourself.' On these two commandments hang all the Law and the Prophets" (Matthew 22:37–40).

If these summaries seem too general, other

Bible texts use the phrase "the will of God" and provide greater detail about how God wants His children to live. Following are seven aspects of our everyday lives that concern God:

- *Sacrifice.* "I beseech you therefore, brethren, by the mercies of God, that you present your bodies a living sacrifice, holy, acceptable to God, which is your reasonable service. And do not be conformed to this world, but be transformed by the renewing of your mind, that you may prove what is that good and acceptable and perfect will of God" (Romans 12:1–2). When believers grasp the first eleven chapters of Romans, which describe all that God has done to save them, they should make a presentation of themselves to God in complete devotion to Him. Unlike the Old Testament animal sacrifices, which were offered to God through death, believers are to offer themselves to God through a dedicated life. This involves a separation from the world's evil influence. It also means a renewing of how we think as we learn God's truth, allowing ourselves to be affected by the Bible's holy influence. As our own sacrifice

deepens, we can say what we had never able
to say before: that God's will is best. It is
good, acceptable, and perfect!

- *Singing, supplication, and showing thanks.*
  "Rejoice always, pray without ceasing,
  in everything give thanks; for this is
  the will of God in Christ Jesus for you"
  (1 Thessalonians 5:16–18). These three
  commands describe inner attitudes that
  express our relationship to God. They reveal
  that Christians should be joyful, prayerful,
  and grateful people. Notice the emphasis:
  "always. . .without ceasing. . .in everything."
  The point is that believers should
  continually be involved in these positive
  activities if they are to do God's will. As
  Bible scholar and writer D. Edmond
  Hiebert said poetically, "If the dove of
  Christian joy is continually to mount
  upward it must fly on the wings of prayer
  and thanksgiving."

- *Sanctification.* "For this is the will of God,
  your sanctification: that you should abstain
  from sexual immorality" (1 Thessalonians
  4:3). The word *sanctification* as it's used in

this verse means to be set apart to God
for a lifestyle characterized by holiness.
His will is that sexual activity remain
pure—by staying within the boundaries
of His ordained institution of marriage
("holy matrimony"). For intimate physical
expressions of love, God established both
marriage boundaries (see Hebrews 13:4)
and gender boundaries (see Romans
1:26–27) so that human couples would
bring blessing to their families and produce
glory for Him. When sin contaminates sex,
people reject these borders and selfishly
seek their own will and pleasure. What
pleases God and one's spouse is left behind.

• *Submission.* "For this is the will of God,
that by doing good you may put to silence
the ignorance of foolish men" (1 Peter
2:15). In this passage, Peter urges believers
to develop a good public testimony by
being productive and pleasant citizens
who obey the man-made laws of the land.
By doing so, Christians can counteract
the criticism (often unjust) of those who
ridicule believers and their gospel message.
Submitting to the laws of our land protects

us from the humiliation and pain of punishment but is ultimately to honor the Lord (see 1 Peter 2:13–15).

- *Sincerity.* "Bondservants, be obedient to those who are your masters according to the flesh, with fear and trembling, in sincerity of heart, as to Christ; not with eyeservice, as men-pleasers, but as bondservants of Christ, doing the will of God from the heart" (Ephesians 6:5–6). Paul wrote this command when slavery was an accepted practice in the Roman Empire. The best twenty-first century comparison is the employment setting—and how sincerely believers act toward those in authority over them. When Christians are evaluated at work, they should have a reputation for diligence and respect. Why be industrious? Paul says that is doing God's will. We should work like we are working for Christ, our heavenly Master (Ephesians 6:9).

- *Suitability.* "Therefore be careful how you walk, not as unwise men but as wise, making the most of your time, because the days are evil. So then do not be foolish, but understand what the will of the Lord is" (Ephesians 5:15–17 NASB). A Christian's behavior is to be suitable for the godly lifestyle described in scripture. And part of that suitability is a thoughtful sense of urgency regarding how we use the time God has given each of us. Wise people understand that evil is gradually eroding their opportunities to serve Christ and win the lost. Nations are closing their borders to the gospel, and individuals are closing their hearts due to the pleasures of sin. If we aren't careful, even those of us who serve as Christ's ambassadors can lose our resolve.

- *Suffering.* "Therefore let those who suffer according to the will of God commit their souls to Him in doing good, as to a faithful Creator" (1 Peter 4:19). According to the apostle Paul, the *normal* Christian life includes suffering for Christ's sake (see Philippians 1:29). How we respond to suffering reveals a lot about us: Though we can't control what happens to us, we can control our reaction. The tendency in hard times is to think that God has abandoned us, that He is somehow unfaithful—which is never the case. Though we certainly don't enjoy suffering, God can use hardships in a sinful world to accomplish His purposes in and through us. We can trust Him as our "faithful Creator," the One who knows what's best for us. God will always be true to His promises, His nature, and His children. Understand that the will of God will never lead you where the grace of God can't keep you.

Though none of us live up to God's standards perfectly, we should still conclude that God's will—as defined in these seven areas—is best. If we find ourselves resisting what God's word says about living the Christian life, let's consider what David wrote in Psalm 19: God's word is "perfect" (that is, flawless, verse 7); "sure" (dependable, verse 7); "right" (leading in a correct way, to the proper goal, verse 8); and "true" (the ultimate standard for what is correct, verse 9).

God's word will always point us to God's will.

Our prayer:

Search me, O God, and know my heart;
try me, and know my anxieties;
and see if there is any wicked way in me,
and lead me in the way everlasting.
PSALM 139:23–24

Questions to Ponder:

1. How does God's moral will differ from His sovereign will?

2. What are some improper views we might have of God's moral will?

3. What is God's desire for unbelievers?

4. How many verses can you name that specifically refer to God's moral will?

4
Discovering the Will of God

Trust in the LORD with all your heart, and lean not on your own understanding; in all your ways acknowledge Him, and He shall direct your paths.

PROVERBS 3:5–6

So now we come to the third aspect of God's will which has been called His "will of direction." This aspect of divine will has also been identified as God's "providential will," because it involves the gradual unfolding of the Lord's plan through His involvement in the circumstances of our lives. Some have called it God's "individual will," because it is His specialized plan and purpose for each believer.

God calls people in different ways and to different experiences to accomplish His purposes. So a legitimate question arises in believers' minds: "What does God want to do with *my* life"?

When Saul, the persecutor of Christians, met Jesus on the road to Damascus and became a Christian himself, his first question was, "Lord, what do You want me to do?" (Acts 9:6). For the man later known as the apostle Paul, the immediate concern was God's will for his life—now that he knew the truth, he would not waste any time in committing himself to God's work.

If we, too, have been saved, the question is the same for us. Learning God's providential will for our own lives rests within each of our hearts. And so our search, like Paul's, begins.

I was once teaching a grandchild some basic rules of chess. As I moved one of my pieces, I was asked, "Grandpa, why did you move there?" I responded, "I've got a plan. You'll see it in a moment, after I make a few more moves!" And so it is with God.

God saves sinners that they might live with Him forever. But right now, He wants to use each believer in a special way, to accomplish His larger plan of calling out a people for His name (see Acts 15:14). We do well to remember that we've been *saved to serve*—in the role and the place of God's choosing.

Paul said repeatedly that he was "called to

be an apostle of Jesus Christ through the will of God" (see 1 Corinthians 1:1; Ephesians 1:1; Colossians 1:1). In a sermon preached in Antioch of Pisidia, Paul said King David had "served his own generation by the will of God" (Acts 13:36). God told the prophet Jeremiah, "Before I formed you in the womb I knew you; before you were born I sanctified you; I ordained you a prophet to the nations" (Jeremiah 1:5). God had a special purpose for the life of each great Bible figure—and He has His plans for us, too.

To accomplish His own purposes, God has placed us strategically in the world. We live in different places, attend different churches, work at different jobs, and have different relatives, friends, and neighbors. Our mission field surrounds us, and God wants to use us as instruments in His hands.

God has given each of us some natural human ability and interest, but He's also provided His children with spiritual abilities called "the gifts of the Spirit." These are distributed "to each one individually as He wills" (1 Corinthians 12:11), and are used to minister to others—whether people we know or not. All believers have a vital role to play in people's lives and an important job to do for their King.

The importance of each believer's role in the body of Christ is illustrated in 1 Corinthians 12:14–20. Paul depicts Christians as parts of a physical body, all working together. If some parts seem insignificant to us, we must recognize that "God has placed the members, each one of them, in the body, just as He desired" (verse 18 NASB).

God might give us a highly visible job, one with a lot of public attention. Or He might keep us behind the scenes, where only He knows what we're contributing. Either way, our attitude should be like the sons of Korah, who served in the Old Testament temple: "I would rather be a doorkeeper in the house of my God than dwell in the tents of wickedness" (Psalm 84:10).

Whatever we do in God's service, we should remember that we are just one piece of the puzzle. But if our piece is missing, the puzzle suffers.

The Importance of Seeking God's Will

The Latin phrase *Deo volente* (sometimes abbreviated D.V.) means "God willing." For centuries, people have used these words to acknowledge God's sovereign control in their lives.

Let's consider three Bible passages that show

how important it is always to seek God's will in our lives:

- The New Testament writer James tells of Christian entrepreneurs who make a business plan involving a sales territory, a specific length of time, and the buying and selling of products to make a profit (see James 4:13). From a dollars-and-cents perspective, the plan sounds good. But from a spiritual standpoint it's incomplete—because God has been totally ignored. These businesspeople were practical atheists, treating God as if He didn't exist.

  This dangerous attitude of self-reliance can affect any of us at some time or another. But we must remember that the poem "Invictus," featuring the famous lines "I am the master of my fate; I am the captain of my soul," doesn't reflect biblical truth!

  James says a complete business plan includes two more points (verses 14–15). First, we must consider that we might not even live to see the next day. Secondly, that possibility should always lead us to a consideration of God's will for our lives.

The reality is that any day could be our last. The rich fool of Jesus' parable (Luke 12) made the same mistake of focusing only on financial matters while ignoring the need to prepare for eternity. This kind of arrogance in our planning is identified as a sin of omission (see James 4:17).

- In 2 Samuel 7, King David wanted to build a temple in Jerusalem to house the ark of the covenant in God's honor. After sharing his plan with his trusted advisor Nathan, the prophet encouraged the king to proceed: "Go, do all that is in your heart, for the LORD is with you" (verse 3).

  It appears, however, that Nathan's eagerness to see a temple caused him to speak prematurely, without consulting God. A temple would indeed be built, but not by David. Later that evening, God communicated *His* will to Nathan, explaining that David—who had been involved in much bloodshed as a warrior— was not to build the temple. The job would fall to David's son Solomon, whose name means "peaceful" (verses 5–16; 1 Chronicles 22:6–16).

Even good, important men like Nathan and David can't be hasty to make decisions. Always seek God in significant matters, asking, "Is our plan Your plan?"

• During the reign of the Old Testament king Hezekiah, the powerful Assyrian empire threatened Judah with a military invasion. Rather than trusting God for help, many in Judah preferred a military alliance with neighboring Egypt—which was not God's will. The Lord sent a rebuke through His prophet Isaiah, saying, "Woe to the rebellious children. . .who take counsel, but not of Me, and who devise plans, but not of My Spirit, that they may add sin to sin; who walk to go down to Egypt, and have not asked My advice" (Isaiah 30:1–2).

Judah's misplaced trust was a result of rejecting God's word. The people were tired of Isaiah's messages that contradicted their own plans. Like many today, they wanted messages that were amiable instead of accurate! Isaiah declared that they were "children who will not hear the law of the LORD; who say to the seers, 'Do not see,' and to the prophets, 'Do not prophesy to us right things; speak to us smooth things, prophesy deceits' "(Isaiah 30:9–10).

The people darkened the lamp of God's word, a choice that eventually led to their nation's destruction.

Methods for Discovering God's Will

So how do we actually determine God's will for ourselves?

Some methods for discovering God's will are simply wrong. Some Old Testament methods—such as following spectacular supernatural signs—are now obsolete. But there are practical steps for Christians to follow today when making important decisions. Note that these steps are not like working the combination of a safe—they should be regular aspects of our Christian lives, along with a patient waiting on the Lord.

Let's examine what the Bible says about different methods of seeking His will—methods prohibited, past, and permanent.

Prohibited Methods

Be careful not to look in the wrong places or listen to the wrong people. When Israel prepared to enter the Promised Land, God warned His people to avoid the evil practices of the idolatrous pagan people already there. The people of Canaan were "spiritual" people who sought to know the future by witchcraft, sorcery, and consultations mediums. The Lord called these superstitions "abominations"—and they were a reason He drove the Canaanites out of the land that belonged to Him (see Deuteronomy 18:9–14; Leviticus 25:23). King Saul, desperate for guidance before a battle, resorted to this evil by consulting the witch of Endor (see 1 Samuel 28:7–19). Heathen peoples looked to the stars for guidance (see Jeremiah 10:2), and the Bible writer Luke indicated the involvement of demons in these practices (see Acts 16:16).

Today, people seek messages from spirit guides, psychics, fortune-tellers, palm readings, tarot cards, and astrology, which purports to foretell human experiences through the positions of the constellations.

The prophet Isaiah challenged the influence of these evil techniques with a stunning declaration that pointed people back to God's word: "And when they say to you, 'Seek those who are mediums and wizards, who whisper and mutter,' should not a people seek their God? Should they seek the dead on behalf of the living? To the law and to the testimony! If they do not speak according to this word, it is because there is no light in them" (Isaiah 8:19–20).

Past Methods

God used at least ten unique methods to guide His people in Bible times, but these are now obsolete. On special occasions, God led His people through supernatural means. Other methods were less spectacular but just as effective. As Bible believers, we understand that God can do anything He wills to do—but these temporary methods from the Old Testament and apostolic eras are not to be viewed today as standards for determining God's will. Why? Because we have been given God's completed word and the abiding presence of His Spirit.

The methods God used in the past:

• God led the nation of Israel by a visible symbol of His presence, a pillar of cloud by day and a pillar of fire by night (Psalm 78:14).

- God spoke audibly to lead select servants:
  to Noah (Genesis 6:13–14), to Abram
  (Genesis 12:1–3), to Moses face-to-face
  (Exodus 33:11), and to Elijah in a still
  small voice (1 Kings 19:9–12). These men
  could honestly and literally say, "God spoke
  to me."

- God sent angels to deliver messages:
  God's answer to Daniel's prayer (Daniel
  10:10–14), the Savior's birth announcement
  to shepherds (Luke 2:8–12), directions to
  Philip about where to meet a man to lead
  him to Christ (Acts 8:26–35).

- God sent prophets to deliver specialized
  messages. Hosea declared, "Hear the word
  of the LORD, you children of Israel" (Hosea
  4:1). King Zedekiah asked Jeremiah to ask
  the Lord for His will, and Jeremiah faithfully
  delivered God's exact answer (Jeremiah
  21:1–7). Jonah reluctantly delivered God's
  message to the city of Nineveh, resulting in a
  great revival (Jonah 3:4–10).

- God communicated in dreams, as a rare
  vehicle for divine messages. Jacob's dream

has been referred to as the story of Jacob's ladder (Genesis 28:12–19). Joseph had been called "this dreamer" (Genesis 37:19) and both he (Genesis 41:14–32) and, much later, Daniel (Daniel 2:26–30) were enabled to interpret dreams. The wise men and Joseph, Jesus' earthly father, received warnings through dreams (Matthew 2:12–13).

- God communicated through visions, dream-like sequences for select individuals who were awake. The prophets Isaiah (Isaiah 6) and Daniel (Daniel 10:5–7) both received visions. In the apostolic days, visions also came to Ananias, Cornelius, Peter, and Paul (Acts 9:10; 10:1–20; 16:9).

- God led the wise men with a star. Such guidance occurred only once in scripture, with no explanation as to the exact nature of the phenomenon. Each holiday season, we sing about this marvel as the "star of wonder, star of light" (Matthew 2:9–11).

- God directed Israel through the Urim and Thummim. Though not much is specifically revealed about these small objects, they were kept in the clothing of the Jewish high priest and used only by him to determine God's will (Exodus 28:30).

- God revealed His will through casting lots. The outcome of this procedure was directed by the Lord (Proverbs 16:33). It was used by the tribes of Israel to divide the Promised Land (Joshua 14:1–2), and its last recorded use was by the apostles selecting a replacement for Judas Iscariot (Acts 1:24–26).

- God confirmed His will through a fleece (Judges 6:11–40). This isolated method was actually selected by Gideon rather than God—and apparently tested God's patience, as Gideon begged God, "Do not be angry with me" (6:39).

Gideon had been divinely appointed as a warrior-judge to lead Israel against enemy invaders. He wanted to verify his calling with even further supernatural input, using a fleece.

Some have suggested that Christians imitate Gideon by "putting out a fleece," asking God to communicate His will through special signs of our choosing. But it seems to me if that's what people want, they should ask for the same two signs Gideon did—which few, if any, do. A closer look at the story reveals that we shouldn't test God at all, but rather take Him at His word.

Overall, Gideon is recognized for great faith (Hebrews 11:32), but in this case he displayed great *doubt*. He'd been called through the miraculous appearance of the Angel of the Lord, who consumed an offering by fire and then vanished (Judges 6:12–21)! This in itself was an astonishing confirmation of God's will, but Gideon still rejected God's methods of guidance to make up *his* own. God graciously accommodated Gideon's challenge and performed this sign (verses 36–38).

Gideon's act of testing God with a fleece was a sign of weak faith—it's best to simply take God at His word. This method is never repeated in the Bible, and no scripture encourages the practice.

A Lesson about God's Will from F. B. Meyer

When I was crossing the Irish channel on a starless night I stood on the deck by the captain and asked him, "How do you know Holyhead Harbor on so dark a night as this?" He said, "Do you see those three lights? Those three lights must line up behind each other as one, and when we see them so united we know the exact position of the harbor's mouth." When we want to know God's will, there are three things that always concur—the inward impulse, the word of God, and the trend of circumstances. God in the heart, impelling you forward; God in His book corroborating whatever He says in the heart; and God in circumstances, which are always indicative of His will. Never start until all three agree.

Permanent Methods

Now we can consider some practical, permanent methods by which Christians can discern God's will.

Note this is not a "dispensational" issue—as though all of the Old Testament methods are archaic while the New Testament presents new approaches for believers today. These permanent (and less spectacular) New Testament methods originate in the Old Testament; God intended them for all believers at all times, even if He occasionally chose to use extraordinary methods.

To make these methods easier to remember, I'll present them in alphabetical order as the "ABCs of God's direction":

- *Advisors:* "Where there is no counsel, the people fall; but in the multitude of counselors there is safety" (Proverbs 11:14). Too many mistakes occur when we don't seek helpful advice. Often, other people can see what we can't and point out things that we've overlooked. So, when possible, decision making should be a group effort: "Without counsel plans fail, but with many advisors they succeed" (Proverbs 15:22 ESV).

  An interesting verse about guidance,

Isaiah 30:21 is frequently thought to refer to God's mysterious voice: "Your ears shall hear a word behind you, saying, 'This is the way, walk in it,' whenever you turn to the right hand or whenever you turn to the left." But a closer look at the context reveals the voice is actually that of our teachers, speaking God's wisdom and functioning as wise advisors (see verse 20).

While recognizing the value of others' help, we still need to be careful just *who* we select as advisors. The Psalms begin by describing the person blessed by God: "Blessed is the man who walks not in the counsel of the ungodly" (Psalm 1:1).

- *The Bible:* "Your word is a lamp to my feet and a light to my path" (Psalm 119:105). God's word first lights our way to the cross, where lost sinners find Jesus as Savior. Then it lights the way of God's will for Christian living, so we can "walk as children of light" (Ephesians 5:8). When we live our lives within the God-ordained boundaries of His revealed moral will, He leads us in paths of righteousness.

  Note that the "lamp" mentioned in

Psalm 119 referred to a lantern or flaming torch that provided just enough light to see a few steps ahead, light sufficient to keep people from dangerous obstacles or turns in the road. So it is with the Bible, which keeps us from life's dangers while providing direction day-by-day. It contains examples from history, so we can learn to imitate the good that God's people did while avoiding mistakes that have been made (1 Corinthians 10:11).

Peter, who had heard God's own voice at the Mount of Transfiguration, gave God's *written* word a special emphasis in his second letter to believers. "We have the prophetic word more fully confirmed," Peter said, "to which you will do well to pay attention as to a lamp shining in a dark place" (2 Peter 1:19 ESV).

• *Circumstances:* "They were forbidden by the Holy Spirit to preach the word in Asia. After they had come to Mysia, they tried to go into Bithynia, but the Spirit did not permit them. So passing by Mysia, they came down to Troas. . . . Now after he had seen the vision, immediately we sought

to go to Macedonia, concluding that the
Lord had called us to preach the gospel to
them" (Acts 16:6–8, 10). Paul experienced
occasional roadblocks to his planned
missionary travels, detours that kept him
and his team moving in God's preferred
direction. In this case, Macedonia is where
God wanted Paul and his companions to
establish churches, in cities like Philippi
and Thessalonica.

God opened and closed doors for Paul
(1 Corinthians 16:5–9; 2 Corinthians 2:12),
as He'll often do for us. When, through a
change in circumstances, God modifies our
plans to conform to His, we must be willing
to adjust in the belief that God is leading
us. Remember that "a man's heart plans
his way, but the Lord directs his steps"
(Proverbs 16:9). As the devotional *Our
Daily Bread* once suggested, "Write your
plan in pencil then give God the eraser."

• *Desires:* "I told no one what my God
had put in my heart to do at Jerusalem"
(Nehemiah 2:12). God appointed and
empowered Nehemiah to direct the
rebuilding of Jerusalem's walls. He

attributed his inner compulsion as something that God had put within him and was leading him to do (Nehemiah 7:5).

Decades earlier, God had stirred the hearts of a Jewish remnant, recently freed from Babylonian captivity, to return to Jerusalem to build a second temple (Ezra 1:5; Haggai 1:14). It is God who works in the hearts of believers to guide and empower them to do what pleases Him (Philippians 2:13).

Let's be careful here, though. This subjective form of leading has occasionally been abused to justify sin by people who claimed God was directing their inappropriate behavior. Our desires must conform to God's holiness as stated in scripture. When our desires parallel the permanent methods of God's guidance, we can honestly say that we are experiencing divine promptings. We can testify "I felt led of the Lord to do this."

Many Christians know God's promise of Psalm 37:4: "Delight yourself also in the LORD, and He shall give you the desires of your heart." This is a great promise, but we shouldn't set ourselves up for disappointment by concluding that God has promised to give us *anything* we want. Psalm 37:4 is a conditional promise that connects our desires to our delight in the Lord—who then molds our desires to accept His will. As pastor and author Warren Wiersbe has observed, "This is not a promise for people who want 'things,' but for those who want more of God in their lives."

- *Entreating God:* "Teach me to do Your will, for You are my God; Your Spirit is good. Lead me in the land of uprightness" (Psalm 143:10). The psalm writer David was the man he was because of prayers like this. He recognized his need to be taught and empowered by God to do God's will—and this became his regular prayer request.

Prayer is the *first* thing Christians should pursue in our quest to discover God's will. We are given a great promise in 1 John 5:14 to encourage praying "according to His will": When we do, "He hears us." We can join believers throughout time in prayers like this: "Do not lead us into temptation, but deliver us from the evil one" (Matthew 6:13).

And we can pray the will of God for others, too. The apostle Paul's companion Epaphras was devoted to praying for others about God's direction. It was said of him that he is "always laboring fervently for you in prayers, that you may stand perfect and complete in all the will of God" (Colossians 4:12).

- *Faith in God:* "Trust in the LORD with all your heart, and lean not on your own understanding; in all your ways acknowledge Him, and He shall direct your paths" (Proverbs 3:5–6). Here is another conditional promise—one requiring three actions on our part to secure the Lord's guidance. First, we must have a childlike confidence in God. The blind hymn writer, Fanny Crosby, expressed her faith in these words,

All the way my Savior leads me—
what have I to ask beside?
Can I doubt His tender mercy,
Who through life has been my Guide?
Heavenly peace, divinest comfort,
Here by faith in Him to dwell!

For I know, what-e'er befall me,
Jesus doeth all things well.

Second, we are warned against trusting our mere human insights as the prophet Jeremiah described (Jeremiah 17:5–6). The nineteenth-century British preacher and theologian Charles Bridges said, "The Christian on his knees, as if he cast his understanding away, confesses himself utterly unable to guide his path. But see him in his active life. He carefully improves his mind. . . . It is our plain duty not to neglect our understanding, but to cultivate it diligently in all its faculties."

Finally, the faith that receives God's blessing acknowledges God's presence continually—through prayer, worship, and joyful obedience. Whether our circumstances involve difficulty or blessing, Jesus Christ must be our life's focus.

When all these conditions are met, we can expect God's guidance into His good and perfect plan for our lives. If we trust Him as our Savior to deliver our souls, we can trust Him as our Shepherd to guide our lives.

As we noted earlier, most of God's will is already revealed in scripture. If we follow these permanent methods for discovering God's will, He will lead us into His special plan for our lives. We may have to "wait, I say, on the LORD" (Psalm 27:14), but trust that He knows just what to do and when to do it.

As God's plan for your life becomes clearer, thank Him, praise Him, and serve Him with gladness.

Our prayer:

Show me Your ways, O LORD; teach me Your paths.
Lead me in Your truth and teach me,
for You are the God of my salvation;
on You I wait all the day.
PSALM 25:4–5

Questions to Ponder:

1. How could the business plan in James 4:13 be improved?

2. What methods for telling the future are divinely prohibited?

3. What supernatural methods has God used in the past to guide believers?

4. What permanent methods does God use today to guide all believers?

5
Suffering and the Will of God

Let those who suffer according to the will of God
commit their souls to Him in doing good,
as to a faithful Creator.
1 PETER 4:19

As I wrote this book, Japan was devastated by an earthquake and tsunami, the Mississippi River overflowed, tornadoes raced through the American Midwest, and wildfires scorched Arizona. The toll in lives was inconceivable; many other people were injured or missing; possessions were gone; survivors would never be the same. Every day, people experience private, individual hardships—relational problems, disease, death. Christians around the world are mocked, beaten, imprisoned, and killed. And the age-old questions arise: "How could a good, loving, and powerful God let this happen? Why do people suffer? Is this somehow my fault?

What do I do now?"

Grieving people in scripture asked similar questions. Gideon, upset about the oppression of Israel, complained, "If the LORD is with us, why then has all this happened to us? And where are all His miracles?"(Judges 6:13). Naomi, who lost a husband and two sons in a short time, said, "Do not call me Naomi; call me Mara [Bitter], for the Almighty has dealt very bitterly with me" (Ruth 1:20). Jacob, who thought his son Joseph was dead and knew his son Simeon was in an Egyptian prison, cried in despair, "All these things are against me" (Genesis 42:36).

The Bible provides general information about God's purpose in tragedies—but some answers will not be available this side of heaven. No human being has the wisdom or authority to say specifically why we suffer, so we look to God's written word for answers. The school of affliction offers many lessons for responding to trials in Christ-honoring ways—unlike King Ahaz, of whom it was said, "Now in the time of his distress King Ahaz became increasingly unfaithful to the LORD" (2 Chronicles 28:22). We should instead imitate the priest Eli, who humbly said, "It is the LORD. Let Him do what seems good to Him" (1 Samuel 3:18).

The Character of God

To persevere during trials, we should consider what God has revealed about Himself in scripture—and view all the events of our lives through that lens. "Where we see anything of God," said the seventeenth-century English Puritan clergyman Thomas Manton, "we owe nothing but reverence and submission; for He is too strong to be resisted, too just to be questioned, and too good to be suspected."

Ironically, some have attempted to protect God's reputation in a skeptical world by suggesting ideas of God that strip away His divine attributes of omniscience, omnipotence, and sovereignty. These people try to explain suffering as only the result of bad human choices or random upheavals of nature. But Job's three friends learned that God is not pleased to be misrepresented (Job 42:7). The best answers to our questions about God will always be found in biblical revelation—not the human imagination.

What God Says about His Attributes

The Zoroastrian religion of the ancient Persian Empire worshipped two gods: Ahura Mazda, the god of good things, and Ahriman, the god of bad things. Over a century earlier, before Cyrus became emperor of Persia, the true God revealed in a scripture addressed to Cyrus by name, that Jehovah was the only God—sovereign, just, and good. He said, "I form the light and create darkness, I make peace and create calamity; I, the LORD, do all these things" (Isaiah 45:7).

Job understood this truth, even when he lost his wealth and his children to attacks of Satan. Job said, "The LORD gave, and the LORD has taken away; blessed be the name of the LORD" (Job 1:21). When Job also lost his health, he asked rhetorically, "Shall we indeed accept good from God, and shall we not accept adversity?" And the Bible adds, "In all this Job did not sin with his lips'"(Job 2:10).

Centuries after Job, Paul would confirm this two-sided aspect of God's sovereignty by urging believers in Rome to "consider the goodness and severity of God" (Romans 11:22).

People are generally quick to note God's "severity"—even the modern insurance industry refers to natural disasters as "acts of God." Unbelieving critics often pose questions that simply accuse God, and sadly, even many believers struggle to see God's goodness.

Far better to take the view of African

Christians, who frequently live with pervasive poverty and disease. I'm told that a common greeting is "God is good all the time," to which another responds, "All the time God is good." By this they're reminded of this overarching attribute of God in the midst of life's confusing hardships.

In addition to God's goodness, here are several other divine attributes we do well to understand and trust, even before we're faced with a hard situation. God is:

- *All knowing* (Exodus 3:7; Psalm 139:1–6; 147:3–5): He is fully aware of all we experience, and He knows what is best for us.

- *All powerful* (Isaiah 40:25–31): He has the ability to protect us from harm and strengthen us during our troubles.

- *Always present* (Psalm 46:1–11): He will never leave us—so He is always available to help and strengthen us.

- *Wise* (Romans 16:27): He deals with us in ways that exceed our understanding—and gives wisdom as we need it.

- *Loving* (1 Peter 5:6–7): We can approach Him with our problems since He cares for us.

- *Faithful* (Lamentations 3:19–23): He keeps all of His promises and daily continues His work in us.

- *Righteous* (Psalm 145:17): All He does and permits is righteous. He is never unfair or evil and is unworthy of criticism.

What God Says about His Actions

God's actions always accord with His nature—so even when His people suffer, it's ultimately for our good and His glory. Note these promises of scripture:

- *He makes all things work out for good* (Romans 8:28; Genesis 50:20). It is a great certainty—for faithful believers—that God brings good out of evil, light out of darkness, and life out of death in His own time and His own way. This is God's providential work on behalf of His children.

- *He limits our trials* (1 Corinthians 10:13). By being faithful to this promise—by His wise management of the length and intensity of our trials—God enables us to endure. And, with every temptation, He provides an escape route.

- *He suffers with us* (Isaiah 63:9). As with any good father who looks out for his children, God has a sympathetic concern for us in our trials. He knows every heartache we've felt, every tear we have shed (Psalm 56:8).

The Purposes of God

The Christian apologist C. S. Lewis wrote in *The Problem of Pain*, "God whispers to us in our pleasures, speaks in our conscience, but shouts in our pain: it is His megaphone to rouse a deaf world."

During hard times, it can be difficult to understand what God is doing. President Abraham Lincoln admitted this toward the end of the Civil War, during his second inaugural address. Lincoln said, "The Almighty has His own purposes."

But God *is* at work during our suffering—

and He invites us to take the occasion of our trials to ask Him for wisdom (James 1:3–5). Such wisdom will help us see that calamity is not always the result of our own sin (see Job 4:7–8; John 9:1–3; Acts 28:3–6). As Jesus noted, the most important question is not how a person suffers, but whether they're prepared for death by personal repentance (Luke 13:1–5).

In some cases, God has revealed His purposes in human suffering. Let's review several scriptures that lay a foundation for understanding whatever suffering we may be experiencing personally. Following are ten reasons for why people suffer—two are related to unbelievers and the rest to Christians:

People Suffer Because They Are Sons of Adam

These reasons for suffering encompass every human being, all of whom are sinners because they are all descendants of Adam.

- *The curse of sin:* God announced to the first man, Adam, that because of his sin the world would fall under a curse and humans would experience the pains of death (Genesis 3:17–19). Under this curse, evil passes from generation to generation and sin abounds with awful effect (Romans 5:12), so everyone is subjected to suffering and misery. Growing old and dying are simply the wages of our sinfulness (Romans 6:23). The apostle Paul explained that the entire earth is also affected by human sin: "Creation was subjected to futility. . .the bondage of corruption [and] groans and labors with birth pangs" (Romans 8:20–22).

- *The retribution of God:* "Beloved, do not avenge yourselves, but rather give place to wrath; for it is written, 'Vengeance is Mine, I will repay,' says the Lord" (Romans 12:19). This suffering is related to the hardest unbelievers who reject God and harm His people. When others hurt us, our natural tendency is for revenge—but God's "beloved" children are told to trust *Him* to deal with evil people in His time and in His way. For those who have caused Christians to suffer, a payday will come—individually and in the global end-time day of vengeance described in 2 Thessalonians 1:6–9.

People Suffer Because They Are Sons of God

Most people can say why bad people suffer—but it's a harder question when Christians experience hardships. In every individual trial, God probably has multiple purposes which He may or may not reveal to us this side of heaven. People may suffer for:

- *The verification of their faith:* "In this you greatly rejoice, though now for a little while, if need be, you have been grieved by various trials, that the genuineness of your faith, being much more precious than gold that perishes, though it is tested by fire, may be found to praise, honor, and glory at the revelation of Jesus Christ" (1 Peter 1:6–7). Bible commentator Alan Stibbs has said, "Just as men use fire to distinguish true gold from counterfeit, so God uses trials to distinguish genuine faith from superficial profession." Our endurance through the acid test of trials contributes to the assurance of our salvation.

- *The production of spiritual fruit:* "We also glory in tribulations, knowing that tribulation produces perseverance; and perseverance, character; and character, hope" (Romans 5:3–4). Bible scholar A. T. Robertson has said, "It is one thing to submit to or to endure tribulations without complaint, but it is another to find ground for glorifying in the midst of them as Paul exhorts here." To experience spiritual joy in trials, we must recognize that they are part of God's plan to purify us like precious metals in a refiner's fire, (Psalm 66:10–11; Isaiah 48:10). Then He will be able to see His own image reflected in us. Since God's discipleship program clearly includes personal tribulation, we should expect it, prepare for it, patiently endure it, and rejoice in what it produces.

• *The prevention of personal sin:* "Lest I should be exalted above measure by the abundance of the revelations, a thorn in the flesh was given to me, a messenger of Satan to buffet me, lest I be exalted above measure" (2 Corinthians 12:7). God designs some trials to be a deterrent to sin. Though the apostle Paul prayed for deliverance, his "thorn in the flesh" was not removed. Instead, Paul learned about God's sustaining grace and testified, "When I am weak, then am I strong" (2 Corinthians 12:10).

- *The correction for personal sin:* "For he who eats and drinks in an unworthy manner eats and drinks judgment to himself, not discerning the Lord's body" (1 Corinthians 11:29). The church ritual known as "the Lord's table" (or Communion) is a serious matter to God. As the Corinthian church carelessly abused the Communion experience, God responded with discipline. This kind of discipline is an evidence of His love and our sonship, as the author of Hebrews reminded believers. God wants His children to partake of His holiness (Hebrews 12:5–11).

- *The instruction in God's word:* "It is good for me that I have been afflicted, that I may learn Your statutes" (Psalm 119:71). Unlike many people, this psalm writer viewed his troubles as "good" because through them he had learned obedience. We can learn much by studying the Bible, but—because of our sinful human tendencies—some lessons must be learned the hard way. The psalmist's own testimony was this: "Before I was afflicted I went astray, but now I keep Your word" (verse 67).

- *The redemption of sinners:* Sometimes, Christians experience a trouble we might call "spiritual labor pain" so sinners can be born again. The apostle Paul wrote to believers in Philippi, "The things which happened to me have actually turned out for the furtherance of the gospel" (Philippians 1:12). What things? Paul was under house arrest of the Roman government, which gave him witnessing opportunities with his guards and others he might not otherwise have met (verse 13; Acts 28:30–31).

- *The identification with Christ:* "Beloved, do not think it strange concerning the fiery trial which is to try you, as though some strange thing happened to you; but rejoice to the extent that you partake of Christ's sufferings. . . . Yet if anyone suffers as a Christian, let him not be ashamed, but let him glorify God in this matter"

(1 Peter 4:12–13, 16). In the Beatitudes, Jesus said this kind of suffering was being "persecuted for righteousness' sake"— which results in a great heavenly reward (Matthew 5:10). Later, Jesus prepared the disciples for His departure by saying, "I chose you out of the world, therefore the world hates you. . . . If they persecuted Me, they will also persecute you" (John 15:19–20; see also 2 Timothy 3:12).

- *The glorification of God:* "This sickness is not unto death, but for the glory of God, that the Son of God may be glorified through it" (John 11:4). Lazarus, the dear friend of Jesus, died soon after becoming sick. The reason for his sickness was not suffering and death but that God would be glorified when Jesus raised Lazarus from the dead. In any suffering, we should try to glorify God—but when He provides swift and special deliverance, we should shout praise to His name (John 9:2–3, 35–38)!

Suffering That Inspired a Song

Horatio Spafford had planned a family trip to Europe, but when a business emergency arose, he sent his wife, Anna, and their four daughters ahead with plans to follow them across the Atlantic as soon as possible. On November 22, 1873, in the middle of the sea, the women's ship collided with another and 226 people—including the four Spafford girls—drowned. Upon her arrival in Wales, Anna sent her husband a heartbreaking telegram: "Saved alone." Horatio immediately sailed for England to join his grief-stricken wife, and as his ship passed the approximate location where his daughters had drowned, he felt the comfort of God that enabled him to write these beloved hymn lyrics:

> *When peace like a river*
> *attendeth my way,*
> *When sorrows like sea billows roll,*
> *Whatever my lot, Thou hast*
> *taught me to say,*
> *It is well, it is well with my soul.*

The Comfort of God

When we feel like making a spiritual 911 call, it's encouraging to know that our God is called the "God of all comfort" (2 Corinthians 1:3). When troubles bring deep distress or last so long that we feel we've been forgotten (Psalm 42:9), we can follow the psalmist's counsel: "Why are you cast down, O my soul? . . . Hope in God" (Psalm 42:11). Like the biblical king Jehoshaphat, we can pray, "We do not know what to do, but our eyes are upon You" (2 Chronicles 20:12).

Jesus spoke comforting words to suffering and fearful people, reassuring them of their value to God, the heavenly Father who is involved in even the smallest details of our lives (Matthew 10:29–31).

Someday, in heaven, God will remove all the things that cause pain, wiping away all tears and bestowing eternal comfort. Even in the present, God uses many means to comfort us:

- *His Spirit of truth:* The divine "Comforter" (KJV) comes alongside believers to permanently live with them (John 14:16); to give assurance of God's love (Romans 5:5) and assurance of our salvation (Romans 8:16); and to pray for them (Romans 8:26–27).

- *His word:* "Remember the word to Your servant, upon which you have caused me to hope. This is my comfort in my affliction" (Psalm 119:49–50). The suffering try many things for relief, and some can help us temporarily. But the psalm writer found lasting comfort for his soul in learning and trusting God's living word (see also Romans 15:4).

- *His people:* God "comforts us in all our tribulation, that we may be able to comfort those who are in any trouble, with the comfort with which we ourselves are comforted by God" (2 Corinthians 1:4). The heavenly comfort we experience is designed to be shared. When we find others who need relief, we should do what we can to bring them comfort.

- *His plan for our future:* "For I consider that the sufferings of this present time are not worthy to be compared with the glory which shall be revealed in us" (Romans 8:18). Our eternal life in heaven will be so magnificent that when compared to the hardships that we currently (and temporarily) endure, a comparison is insignificant (see also 2 Corinthians 4:17).

True Stories of God's Comfort

It may be hard to believe that God's will can include suffering. But three stories—from my own circle of friends—show it is possible to triumph through tragedy by God's comfort.

A Story of Suffering and Joy

When I see Crisi, I'm always greeted with a joyful smile. This young woman has taught me what it means to "rejoice in the Lord always."

As a twelve-year-old in 1992, Crisi was involved in a terrible sledding accident that broke her neck. She spent seven weeks lying motionless in a hospital bed, six months in a rehab center, and the rest of her life in a wheelchair. At first it was unclear whether she would live through the injuries. For some time, Crisi needed home-care from her family and visiting nurses. Now, she is classified as an incomplete quadriplegic with minimal movement.

Crisi says being raised in a Christian home, by solid parent role models, prepared her for this lifelong trial. Fellowship with God was a way of life from early on, and though Crisi says she's never had depression or bitterness toward God, she admits to questioning whether her situation was "fair"—especially as she watched her high school friends having fun. But Crisi believes God answered her question of "why?" with John 10:10, in which Jesus says, "I have come that they may have life, and that they may have it more abundantly." God said to Crisi, "My plan of abundant life for you is better than just having fun."

In early 2004, Crisi married. Her father pushed her wheelchair down the aisle before giving her away. After the ceremony, when the minister presented the new couple, the groom leaned over to kiss his bride, then lifted Crisi out of her chair and carried her to the back of the sanctuary amid a great celebration!

Crisi has touched many lives besides mine. Today she says with contentment, "This is my life. This is the plan that God had for me."

A Story of Suffering and Forgiveness

In the year 2000, tragedy shocked our community when a seventeen-year-old girl named Elizabeth was murdered. Her parents—my friends Jeff and Becki—were awakened early one morning by police, who asked about Elizabeth and a friend's whereabouts. In time, authorities determined that the girls had been abducted—and that Elizabeth had been killed.

They learned the terrible news at the emergency room of the local hospital. An hour later, Jeff and Becki returned home to tell their three sons. The boys sat on a couch as Jeff knelt before them and said through tears, "Your sister has been murdered—and we are going to pray for the salvation of the man who did this."

The first time the family personally saw the killer was in a courtroom filled with television cameras. "This young man, who sat weeping with his head hanging, looked like the empty shell of a man who had been used by Satan and then thrown away," Jeff said. "I then felt the forgiving compassion of Christ who prayed from the cross, 'Father, forgive them for they know not what they do.'"

Ironically, these beautiful feelings of forgiveness created a type of guilt in Jeff when compared to his affectionate devotion to his daughter. But during the trial's sentencing, when the judge permitted each of the grieving parents to speak directly to the killer, they said, "We forgive you because God commands it."

Becki says the family still lives with the tragedy every day. But when they ask God "why?", they believe He answers, "It's not for you to ask 'why?' but to trust Me."

A Story of Suffering and Hope

I've seen different believers face death and say with the apostle Paul, "For to me, to live is Christ, and to die is gain" (Philippians 1:21). Most recently, I watched my friend Dale battle cancer for five months before dying in April 2011. The initial diagnosis—that the cancer was treatable—was hopeful, but Dale quickly learned that the disease was terminal. Still, he maintained such a positive attitude that some people seemed almost annoyed by his response to the trial. Dale's wife, Joy, says he told her, "We can do this the world's way or the Lord's way—let's honor God." Together, they did.

Dale and I attended the same church, where I serve as a Bible teacher. Toward the end of his fifty-two years, as I visited in his hospital room, Dale became the teacher and I the student— he taught me how to die with peace, speaking of trusting Christ's plan for his life. Facing the prospect of imminent death, Dale was thoughtful about the things of God. "This is the life that God gave me and I have to live it," he said. Joy says Dale's attitude helped to prepare family members for his passing.

On Dale's last good day he said, "What I'm going through is nothing compared to what Jesus did at the cross." Today, his tombstone bears the inscription, "Romans 8"—which includes the encouraging truth that nothing "shall be able to separate us from the love of God which is in Christ Jesus our Lord" (verse 39).

May God give us grace to say, like Job, "Though He slay me, yet will I trust Him" (Job 13:15). Remember that our story is never over until we reach the throne of God.

Our prayer:

Make us glad for as many days
as you have afflicted us,
and for as many years as we have seen evil.
PSALM 90:15 ESV

Questions to Ponder:

1. Does any person have authority to tell us specifically why we are suffering?

2. What attributes of God are important to understand during trials?

3. What are some of the Bible's reasons for suffering?

4. How does God comfort sufferers?

6
My Will and the Will of God

*"I have found David, the son of Jesse, a man after
My own heart, who will do all My will."*
ACTS 13:22

Like everyone else, King David was a sinner.
But he possessed a reputation as a man who was
always tender toward God. We have an extensive
record of his sorrow for sin and his prayers of
repentance (Psalms 32, 51). David learned hard
lessons of reaping trouble from the sins he had
sown. But even this truth is a testimony to the
grace of God in David's life. As Bible scholar
Merrill Unger has written, "The errors by which
[David] is carried away stand out prominently
just because of their rarity."

From his youth, David showed evidence of a
heart devoted to the Lord. When God directed
the prophet Samuel to anoint Israel's future king
from among the sons of Jesse, Samuel made

outward appearance his priority for a national leader. But God told the prophet, "The Lord does not see as man sees; for man looks at the outward appearance, but the Lord looks at the heart" (1 Samuel 16:7).

David displayed a heart of courage, when he fought the giant Goliath for God's honor. David showed a heart of worship in his desire to build a temple for God. But he is remembered in the New Testament for a heart to complete God's will: "After he had served his own generation by the will of God, fell asleep" (Acts 13:36).

What does it mean to be a man or woman after God's own heart? The answer, in part, involves our understanding of God's will and our desire to complete it. People after God's heart seek God's will. They learn it. They fulfill it.

David's epitaph is something we should aspire to. God looks for people like David, those with a zeal for God's will. As David's descendant Jesus said, "My food is to do the will of Him who sent Me, and to finish His work" (John 4:34).

Act Now

There is no shortage of books on God's will. Clearly, the Bible itself is a book that reveals

God's will. We have plenty of information on the subject—what we need now is *action*. God wants people who will *do* His will, though many, sadly, won't.

Some Reject God's Will

Some people want nothing to do with God's revealed will regarding His way of salvation and what pleases Him. Some are content to be outwardly religious; others fall away from this "religion" altogether. The Bible gives examples of every type of rejection:

- *"Their heart is far from Me"* (Matthew 15:8). In the time of Christ, this was Jesus' evaluation of those people who had the appearance of doing God's will but viewed their religious traditions as more important than a true relationship with God. They were personally religious and conducted elaborate worship services— but their practices were purely external, never affecting their hearts. Some of their manmade rules even violated God's word (verses 1–6). Jesus called this religious hypocrisy (verses 7–9).

- *They "rejected the will of God for themselves"* (Luke 7:30). As forerunner of the Messiah, John the Baptist preached a baptism of repentance in preparation for Jesus' coming. Sinners—including the socially-despised group known as the tax collectors—flocked to listen to John and be baptized. Having received God's forgiveness, these tax collectors publicly defended God's choice to accept them. On the other hand, the Pharisees—the proud religious leaders of the day—refused to admit their own sin or need for repentance. In rejecting John's message and baptism, they were actually rejecting God's will.

- *"O Jerusalem, Jerusalem. . .you were not willing!"* (Matthew 23:37). During the last week of the Lord's life, it was clear that Israel had rejected Him—just like the nation had rejected previous prophets sent to them. Jesus came to the people, but the people would not come to Him. The Lord's lament was an indication of His will and desire to save sinners—He was willing to save them, but they were not willing to be saved. Instead, as they had done before, they reacted violently to God's offer of mercy.

- *"Do you also want to go away?"* (John 6:67). Jesus had many more than twelve disciples—though one time, a large group of them decided to stop following Him and left. Jesus then asked the Twelve about *their* commitment. If we're ever tempted to abandon Christ, we would do well to remember Peter's answer: "Lord, to whom shall we go? You have the words of eternal life" (John 6:68). Many reject God's will by forsaking His Son, but there will always be those who endure to the end.

Some Resist God's Will

Some people start out following God's will but later oppose it. They fight for their own will to be done rather than God's. The results of this battle are disastrous.

- *"They did not wait for His counsel"* (Psalm 106:13). Soon after the Israelites miraculously crossed the Red Sea, they became impatient with God's plan for their nation.

They complained that it would have been better to stay in Egypt, since God had provided only manna in the desert. So God provided flocks of quail for meat. The people received what they wanted, but also something they weren't expecting: God's righteous judgment by way of a plague (Numbers 11).

C. S. Lewis wrote in *The Great Divorce*, "There are only two kinds of people in the end: those who say to God, 'Thy will be done,' and those to whom God says, in the end, '*Thy* will be done.'" Sometimes God does let people have their own way—to their own destruction.

• *"What are you doing here, Elijah?"* (1 Kings 19:9, 13). God asked His prophet this question after the great victory over the prophets of Baal at Mount Carmel in 1 Kings 18. After the event, the evil queen Jezebel threatened Elijah's life—and in fear he ran to hide in a cave at Mount Horeb. Overwhelmed with discouragement, fearful that he would lose his life, Elijah was not where God wanted him to be. He forgot the truth spoken by missionary David

Livingstone—that we are invincible until our work is complete. Always remember that the best place to be is in the center of God's will.

- *"Jonah arose to flee. . .from the presence of the LORD"* (Jonah 1:3). God had called Jonah to be a missionary to Nineveh, capital city of the brutal Assyrian Empire. Prejudiced against the Assyrians, Jonah ran in the opposite direction, trying to get as far away as he possibly could. A "whale" of a treatment got Jonah back on track for God's will. The prophet reluctantly completed his mission, with a bad attitude throughout the entire story. If Jonah himself wrote the Bible book carrying his name, it appears he finally repented of his callous feelings toward lost souls and God's will.

- *"John, departing from them, returned to Jerusalem"* (Acts 13:13). John Mark was an assistant on Paul's first foreign mission trip. But he abruptly deserted the mission, leaving Paul and Barnabas to serve alone. His behavior was contrary to God's will, since "it is required in stewards that one be found faithful" (1 Corinthians 4:2). The reason for John Mark's delinquency is not stated, but we are told about the trouble that followed: a sharp disagreement occurred between Paul and Barnabas over Mark's involvement in a second planned trip. Unable to agree, Paul and Barnabas went their separate ways to serve the Lord (Acts 15:39–41). In His power and wisdom, God brought good out of this trouble—now there were *two* mission teams serving. Happily, all parties were eventually reconciled (1 Corinthians 9:6; 2 Timothy 4:11).

Some Do God's Will

Some people see their need of salvation and believe in Christ. Then they begin a life of following Jesus—learning His will in the Bible, offering to God the use of their lives day by day. Doing God's will is truly a lifelong commitment.

- *It begins with salvation:* "Whosoever will, let him take the water of life freely" (Revelation 22:17 KJV). In the last chapter of the Bible, a final invitation is given to everyone to receive God's gift of eternal life. This "water of life" is given freely to those who are thirsty for spiritual health (Romans 6:23; Ephesians 2:8–9). When we receive this gift, our will and God's finally agree!

"The world is passing away, and the lust of it; but he who does the will of God abides forever" (1 John 2:17). There is a distinct contrast between the world of perishing unbelievers and the Christians who live forever. The life of true believers is characterized by pleasing God, a pursuit which begins with conversion (1 John 2:12). Careless unbelievers, sadly, are led to destruction by the devil.

- *It continues in Christian living:* "Present your bodies a living sacrifice. . .do not be conformed to this world, but be transformed by the renewing of your mind" (Romans 12:1–2). As Paul finishes the doctrinal part of his letter to the Romans, and begins a very practical section on Christian living, he urges a *presentation*—of our lives to God's service; a *separation*—from the evil influences of the world around us; and a *transformation*—of our lives through the effect of learning God's word. As a result, we'll be able to say, "I have proven that God's will, which is my delight, is always best." This change in a person's life will be like that of a caterpillar becoming a butterfly!

There will be times when we must examine ourselves and confess the sin of not doing God's will—just like David, the man after God's own heart, had to do. God is always faithful to restore anyone who is truly repentant, trusting in Christ's cleansing blood: "If we confess our sins, He is faithful and just to forgive us our sins and to cleanse us from all unrighteousness" (1 John 1:9).

If you've made mistakes, don't despair. God restored Peter, who denied Jesus, and John Mark, who deserted his mission work. In the parable of the prodigal son, Jesus taught that God loves and accepts sinners and offers second chances.

"God's Will Became His Will"

Before he was saved by God's grace, John Newton was sinful and self-willed. His life changed dramatically, though, as he devoted himself to doing God's will. Eventually ordained in the Anglican Church, John Newton is perhaps best remembered for writing the hymn "Amazing Grace." In a small cemetery of a churchyard in Olney, England, a large granite tombstone still shows this inscription which Newton wrote for himself prior to his death in 1807: "John Newton, clerk, once an infidel and libertine, a servant of slavers in Africa, was, by the rich mercy of our Lord and Savior Jesus Christ, preserved, restored, pardoned, and appointed to preach the Faith he had long labored to destroy."

Accountability Comes Later

When this life is over, we will all give an account of ourselves to God. Jesus spoke of this in Matthew 25 in His parable of the talents. From this story comes the phrase all believers hope someday to hear from God: "Well done, good and faithful servant" (verses 21, 23).

The American statesman Daniel Webster was once asked for the greatest thought that had ever crossed his mind. His response was, "My accountability to God." Our own anticipation of this coming review at the judgment seat of Christ should motivate us to learn and do the will of God—then we will be prepared for our judgment.

Scripture reveals several truths about this event:

- *Judgment Day is a reality:* "It is appointed for men to die once, but after this the judgment" (Hebrews 9:27). Ultimate judgment is not a favorite topic of conversation, and many seem to believe that if it's ignored, it might go away. But physical death and divine judgment are inseparably connected. Everyone has an appointment with God that cannot be avoided.

- *Jesus Christ will be our Judge:* "And He [Jesus] commanded us to preach to the people, and to testify that it is He who was ordained by God to be Judge of the living and the dead" (Acts 10:42). God gave proof of this by raising Jesus Himself from the dead (Acts 17:30–31). We will be examined by our Creator, who became the Savior, and who will be our righteous Judge.

- *Judgment leads either to rewards or penalties:* Faithful believers can expect a gracious bestowal of rewards. "If the work that anyone has built on the foundation survives, he will receive a reward" (1 Corinthians 3:14 ESV). Unbelievers, on the other hand, will receive God's justice. "And anyone not found written in the Book of Life was cast into the lake of fire" (Revelation 20:15; see also John 3:36). According to John 5:24, the eternal destiny of believers was settled when they were saved and built their life on the foundation of Jesus Christ (see 1 Corinthians 3:11). The Christian's daily life and service for God will then be tested to determine if they are worthy of rewards (3:12–14). Works that fail this divine test will result in losing rewards—but the person will not lose salvation. As an act of worship, then, all rewards will be returned to Jesus Christ in recognition that our victory is because of Him (Revelation 4:10–11).

- *Pastors and teachers will receive special scrutiny:* "My brethren, let not many of you become teachers, knowing that we shall receive a stricter judgment" (James 3:1; see also Hebrews 13:17). Teaching God's word is a serious matter. This warning is designed to encourage teachers to perform their task earnestly—and to *discourage* the unqualified from trying. Jesus' words in Luke 12:48 apply: "Everyone to whom much is given, from him much will be required."

- *All believers will give an account of themselves:* "So then each of us shall give account of himself to God" (Romans 14:12). In the context of Romans 14, we shouldn't be critical of other Christians since our own life will be under review by Jesus Himself. We won't give an account of anyone but ourselves for the decisions we have personally made. We do well to judge

ourselves now to prepare for that day
(2 Corinthians 5:9–10; 13:5). If we had
to give an account of our lives today, what
would we say?

The last book of the Bible begins and ends
with an emphasis on Jesus' return, which sets
this final judgment into motion. In writing the
Revelation of Jesus Christ, John says, "Behold
He is coming" in the seventh verse of the first
chapter, then quotes Jesus Himself three times
in the last chapter: "I am coming quickly"
(22:7, 12, 20). In 22:12, Jesus adds, "My reward
is with Me, to give to every one according to
his work."

Bible scholar John MacArthur has noted that
early Christians believed Jesus could return at
any moment (a possibility we call "imminence"),
but they never attempted to guess at a date. "Not
knowing when He might return," MacArthur
writes, "they wisely lived prepared for and
hoping for Jesus' return at any moment."

The Clock Is Ticking

In light of Jesus' return, the Bible urges us to use
our remaining time wisely—because we are all

running out of it. As some have said, "Time's a wastin'."

The apostle Paul called believers to shake off laziness and spiritual dullness, to view our lives in the way God does. "Do this, knowing the time, that now it is high time to awake out of sleep," Paul said, "for now our salvation is nearer than when we first believed" (Romans 13:11).

The clock is ticking. The world moves ever closer to the return of Christ and His judgment. So Paul suggests that believers "put on the Lord Jesus Christ" (Romans 13:14), which is a way of saying to live the rest of your life as Jesus lived His. If we followed that advice, what changes would we need to make?

The apostle Peter followed Paul's lead by saying a Christian "no longer should live the rest of his time in the flesh for the lusts of men, but for the will of God. For we have spent enough of our past lifetime in doing the will of the Gentiles" (1 Peter 4:2–3). Our human lives are divided into the time before conversion and the time after it. The concern now is for what remains, that we devote that time to doing God's will.

Unbelievers will view our lifestyle change as odd—and may even mock our stand for Christ. Don't let that intimidate you. Remember that in the future everyone will answer to Christ and "give an account to Him who is ready to judge the living and the dead" (1 Peter 4:5). And that won't be long. As Peter says, "the end of all things is at hand" (1 Peter 4:7).

The Longing of a Heart

The author of the book of Hebrews offers a beautiful prayer for its readers, that the good work God began in their lives would be completed:

Now may the God of peace who brought up our Lord Jesus from the dead, that great Shepherd of the sheep, through the blood of the everlasting covenant, make you complete in every good work to do His will, working in you what is well pleasing in His sight, through Jesus Christ, to whom be glory forever and ever. Amen.
HEBREWS 13:20–21

This benediction is full of great truths. The specific request is that the risen Christ will work in us to make us complete in understanding and doing God's will. Jesus' work in our lives involves peace, power, and pleasing God.

- *Peace:* The prayer is addressed to "the God of peace," the great Peacemaker who made peace for lost sinners through the blood of Jesus. God wants us to be peacemakers, as well, bringing the lost to Christ and enjoying harmony in our Christian fellowships.

- *Power:* God's immense power raised Jesus—our great Shepherd—from the dead. Now He lives for His sheep, continuing His work in them and finally leading them to glory. Like any shepherd, Jesus' strength and ability protect and keep His sheep, "for without Me you can do nothing" (John 15:5).

- *Pleasing God:* The prayer acknowledges God's "working in you what is pleasing in His sight." The ultimate effect of our life should be like that of Enoch, who "pleased God" (Hebrews 11:5).

Let's make this our prayer for ourselves and our fellow Christians. Let's thank God for what He has accomplished so far in our lives and pray that His work will continue—so that His will is done on earth as it is in heaven.

Our prayer:

*So teach us to number our days,
that we may apply our hearts unto wisdom.*
PSALM 90:12 KJV

Questions to Ponder:

1. If David committed such great sin,
    how can he be called a "man after
    God's own heart"?

2. Why do people resist God's will?

3. Why are the heavenly rewards
    (portrayed as "crowns") given back
    to Christ?

4. How can Christians help each other
    learn and do the will of God?

Scripture Index

Other Books by Robert M. West

How to Study the Bible
ISBN 978-1-59789-706-8 /
Paperback / 96 pages / $1.49

This helpful guide provides a brief, concise overview of personal Bible study for the layperson. Long-time Bible teacher Robert M. West gives insight into the types, tools, and techniques of personal study, offering both practical guidance and encouragement to pursue the command of 2 Timothy 2:15—"Be diligent to present yourself approved to God as a workman who does not need to be ashamed, accurately handling the word of truth."

*THE TEN COMMANDMENTS—
THEN AND NOW*
ISBN 978-1-60260-702-6 /
Paperback / 160 pages / $2.99

Most everyone's heard of the Ten Commandments, but what are they really all about? This intriguing study views God's ancient law, handed down to Moses at Mount Sinai, from the perspective of twenty-first century Christian faith: *The Ten Commandments* contain both timeless moral laws and rules that help us understand and relate to God.

Available wherever Christian books are sold.